asiannoodles

ALSO BY NINA SIMONDS:

CHINA EXPRESS

CLASSIC CHINESE CUISINE

CHINA'S FOOD

CHINESE SEASONS

Nina Simonds

Asian Noodles

DELICIOUSLY SIMPLE DISHES TO TWIRL, SLURP, AND SAVOR

PHOTOGRAPHS BY CHRISTOPHER HIRSHEIMER

PHOTO COLLAGES BY ANN FIELD

HEARST BOOKS

NEW YORK

Acknowledgments

SO MANY PEOPLE HAVE CONTRIBUTED to this book's completion, yet space is limited and it's impossible to thank them all here. Nonetheless, the following deserve special mention:

Françoise Fetchko and Julie Lutts, dear friends and fellow cooks, who tested and retested the recipes and never lost their enthusiasm or humor. Farina Achuck also deserves mention for her invaluable help.

Debbie and Richie Lawrence and Piia Kairento, my beloved Jesse-sitters, who made my travels for noodle research possible.

Don Rose and Arthur Mann, who never tired of tasting still *more* noodles.

In Japan, Paul Sasaki, Peter Barakan, Mayumi Yoshida, and James soba-master Udesky; in Ann Arbor, Lucy Seligman; and in New York City, Nobuo Kobari at Honmura An—who all led me to great noodle shops.

In Hong Kong, T. C. Lai, Margaret Sheriden, and Clayton Parker, who were terrific noodle-sharing partners.

In Vietnam, Annabel Jackson-Doling, Rose Earhart, and Patricia Greenfield, who gave great tips and insights.

Rose Schwartz, dear friend, who lent endless support and legal expertise.

At William Morrow, special thanks to Kathleen Hackett, my editor, for her unflagging dedication and enthusiasm. Ann Bramson, Judith Sutton, and Linda Kocur also helped to make this book a success. And Maureen and Eric Lasher were indispensable in its conception.

At *Ph*.D my warmest thanks to Clive Piercy, and to Michael Hodgson for his superb design sense, unerring musical taste, and dry wit; Cindy Nelson at Black and Copper for her input at the initial stages, and Ann Field for her beautiful collages.

Thanks to Christopher Hirsheimer for the stunning photographs, and Cathy Young and Corinne Trang, talented and skilled cooks.

I am extremely grateful to Rux Martin and Barry Estabrook, who first commissioned an article on Asian noodles many years ago.

At *Gourmet*, thanks to Zanne Zakroff Stuart, Kemp Minifie, and Gail Zweigenthal for their continued support and friendship.

At *Eating Well*, Patsy Jamieson and Susan Stuck have been tireless supporters.

At the *Los Angeles Times*, Laurie Ochoa and Russ Parsons have been special colleagues and friends. At *The Boston Globe*, thanks to Fiona Luis and Alison Arnett.

My father and my sister and brothers, their significant others, and their respective broods have all been faithfully supportive.

My dear friends, colleagues, and students continue to nurture, stimulate, and inspire me.

My thanks to you all, and may you be served the longest and most delicious of life's noodles.

NINA SIMONDS

vii

contents

lushest, most appealing ingredients you can find and don't be afraid to substitute freshly made or dried Italian pasta for the Asian varieties (refer to the chart on pages 10–13 for suggested substitutions).

Whatever dishes you do prepare, don't be afraid to show your enthusiasm by slurping your noodles as the Japanese do. Asian noodle dishes, with their fresh ingredients and light sauces, not only are healthy and delicious, but they impart a wish of longevity to those who devour them.

xii

Noodle Basics

As a visit to any Asian market will attest, the number of different noodles is extraordinary and the selection can be daunting. There are, however, some simple clues that will help you determine what you need.

In most Asian markets, noodles usually are grouped by their content. In the dried noodle section, wheat-flour noodles are together, often with egg noodles mixed in. Rice-flour noodles form another section, while cellophane or mung bean starch noodles are organized in another area. Check the refrigerator for fresh varieties; these days both Asian specialty stores and supermarkets are carrying a larger variety of fresh products.

This chapter will guide you in the selection and identification of every type of Asian noodle, with the pictures providing a supplementary key. The accompanying glossary should answer any simple questions regarding background information.

The charts are organized according to ethnic variety, with a basic description of the noodle, specific cooking times for both fresh and dried varieties, a general explanation of the noodle's use, and recommended substitutes. Don't hesitate to use fresh pasta from your supermarket; the substitution guidelines are listed in the charts or in the specific recipes.

The Basic Recipes will give exact instructions on how the noodles should be cooked from their initial stage, whether they are boiled, panfried, or deep-fried. For any type of noodle—wheat or rice, Japanese, Chinese, or Korean—make certain to use a large pot with a generous amount of water. Don't overcook. Asian noodles should often be *al dente*, or tender, just like their Italian cousins, so that their flavor and texture can be fully appreciated.

CELLOPHANE NOODLES

CHINESE EGG NOODLES

FLAT CHINESE EGG NOODLES

LINGUINE

ROUND CHINESE WHEAT-FLOUR NOODLES

FLAT CHINESE WHEAT-FLOUR NOODLES

SPINACH FETTUCCINE

SPRING ROLL WRAPPERS

KOREAN BUCKWHEAT NOODLES

KOREAN SWEET POTATO NOODLES

RAMEN

RICE NOODLES

EXTRA-THIN RICE VERMICELLI

RICE STICKS

RICE PAPER WRAPPERS

SOBA

SOMEN

UDON

The Noodles

HERE IS AN OVERVIEW OF THE ASIAN NOODLES used in this book. Check the chart on pages 10–13 for cooking methods, suggestions for serving, and appropriate substitutions.

CELLOPHANE NOODLES

Also known as bean threads and slippery noodles, cellophane noodles are made from the starch of mung beans, which are most familiar to us as sprouts. Cellophane noodles are translucent in their dried form, but once softened in hot water and cooked, they become gelatinous and transparent. Since they have little or no taste and will absorb the flavors of the ingredients they are cooked with, these noodles are prized mainly for their texture. Cellophane noodles are sold in 1.8-ounce and 3.5-ounce packages.

CHINESE EGG NOODLES

Well-stocked Asian markets usually offer a selection of dried and fresh egg noodles, both thin and thick. Although they are often neon yellow, some of the dried varieties are made without eggs.

These are usually labeled "imitation noodles" and are made with food coloring or dye. If you can't find good-quality Chinese egg noodles, substitute fresh or dried Italian pasta.

CHINESE WHEAT-FLOUR NOODLES

Made with wheat flour and water, these are the oldest form of noodles. In northern China, where they originated, and in select restaurants around the world, they are still made by hand with a soft dough, resulting in a silky texture. Wheat-flour noodles are mainly available dried in Asian markets. They vary in thickness and may be round or flat. The thinnest (Amoy-style or Chinese *somen*) are used in refined soups, whereas the thicker varieties stand up to heartier soups and casseroles. Shrimp-, chicken-,

and crab-flavored dried noodles are also available, but the quality varies dramatically, as does their flavor.

DUMPLING WRAPPERS

Also called wonton skins, *shao mai,* and *gyoza,* dumpling wrappers are widely available in supermarket produce sections and Asian markets. Thin fresh skins are preferable, particularly for steamed dumplings. Generally the round wheat-flour-and-water wrappers are used for boiled and steamed dumplings; square wrappers, made with an egg dough, are reserved for boiled and deep-fried wontons. Some shops offer a deep yellow variety, which may be used for wonton soup. Fresh wrappers will keep for up to a week in the refrigerator and may be frozen up to one month.

KOREAN BUCKWHEAT NOODLES

One of the most popular varieties of noodles with Koreans are the brownish noodles known as *naengmyon,* which are sold dried. They are made with buckwheat flour and potato starch and are slightly chewier than *soba* noodles. They are served cold in a beef broth with slices of Asian pear, but they are also served warm in soups.

KOREAN SWEET POTATO NOODLES

Tangmyon, or sweet potato noodles, are similar to cellophane noodles, and they are often made with mung bean starch. Like cellophane noodles, they become translucent once cooked and will absorb the flavors of the foods they are cooked with. They usually appear in stir-fried dishes, tossed with meat and vegetables.

RAMEN

Many Americans are familiar with Japanese *ramen,* the dried noodles used in "instant" noodle packages. They are usually made with an egg dough. Some Japanese purists consider these noodles Chinese. Ramen are usually served with meat and vegetables in broth. Fresh ramen is not always easy to find so I often substitute fresh or dried Chinese egg noodles or Italian pasta.

RICE NOODLES

The variety of rice stick noodles and vermicelli sold in Asian markets can be overwhelming. Unfortunately, manufacturers do not have a standardized nomenclature: Some extra-thin noodles are labeled "vermicelli"; others are labeled "sticks"; and thicker flat noodles may be called "sticks" as well. You're better off looking at the noodles themselves rather than their names. There are two main types: round and flat.

Extra-Thin Rice Vermicelli

Delicate strands of rice noodles are used by all Asian cooks in soups, salads, and stir-fries. The dried noodles are also deep-fried once in hot oil, then used as "nests" for stir-fried foods. Known as *mi fen* (Chinese), *bun* (Vietnamese), and *sen mee* (Thai), these noodles usually should be softened in hot water before cooking. The thickness varies slightly depending on the manufacturer.

Rice Sticks

Flat dried rice-flour-and-water noodles are available in three main sizes. The thin noodles are primarily used in soups, occasionally in stir-fried dishes. Medium rice sticks (the most popular, *pho,* are best known as a component of the Vietnamese soup of the same name) are all-purpose noodles used in soups, stir-fries, and salads. The slightly wider Thai version are the *jantaboon* noodles. Wide flat rice noodles, sometimes called *sha he fan* on Chinese menus, are best known in stir-fried dishes with meat or seafood and vegetable combinations.

RICE PAPER WRAPPERS

Banh trang, or rice paper wrappers, are translucent sheets, available in both round and triangular shapes, that are made from rice flour, salt, and water. (The unique pattern on the sheets is created when they are dried on bamboo trays.)

7

Although the dried wrappers are brittle, once dipped in hot water, they become soft and pliable in seconds. Traditionally, the round are used for roll-ups and the triangular are used to wrap grilled meats or as wrappers for deep-fried finger foods.

SOBA

The brownish buckwheat *soba* noodles from Japan are becoming more popular as their beguiling, nutty flavor and nutritional value engage the attention of Western cooks. They are rich in protein and fiber. While they are most commonly served cold with a dipping sauce or hot in soups, soba noodles are extraordinarily versatile and lend themselves to salads and stir-fried dishes as well. Soba may also be flavored with green tea (*cha soba*), lemon zest, or black sesame seeds. While a growing number of Western health food companies manufacture and package the noodles, the best-quality soba noodles are still the Japanese brands.

SOMEN

The most delicate Japanese noodles, *somen* are often distinguished by their elegant packaging. They usually are tied with colorful ribbons in neat bundles. Somen are made from a wheat-flour dough with a little oil. Like soba, they are often served cold with a dipping sauce, but they make a delightfully light and delicate garnish for hot soups.

SPRING ROLL SKINS OR LUMPIA WRAPPERS

While Western cooks are most familiar with egg roll wrappers made with a pastalike egg dough, Chinese cooks prefer lacy skins made by rubbing a wheat-flour-and-water dough over a hot grill. They are more delicate for wrapping stir-fried foods, and when deep-fried, they tend to stay crisp. Lumpia wrappers are commonly sold frozen in Asian markets. They should be defrosted and separated, then covered with a damp towel since they tend to dry out quickly.

UDON

Udon are fat, white slippery noodles, appropriate for robust soups and casseroles. They are made from a wheat-flour-and-water dough and may be round, square, or flat. In most recipes, udon noodles are interchangeable with soba noodles and Chinese wheat-flour-and-water noodles.

8

Using the Noodles

ASIAN NOODLES COME IN ALL SHAPES AND SIZES. The same type of noodle may vary dramatically in size and thickness, depending on the manufacturer; thus the cooking time will change accordingly. So, test noodles several times for doneness and revise as necessary. The cooking times listed below for boiled noodles are calculated from the moment the water returns to a boil after the noodles have been added. For some noodles, specific cooking instructions are given.

CHINESE NOODLES

Chinese flour-and-water noodles are mainly used for soups or souplike stews. Egg noodles are used in pan-fried and stir-fried dishes.

NAME/INGREDIENTS	PREPARATION	USE	SUBSTITUTE
THIN EGG NOODLES (wheat flour, egg, and water) *Danmian, xi*	FRESH: Boil for 2½ to 4 minutes DRIED: Boil for 4½ to 5 minutes	panfries, stir-fries	angel hair, vermicelli, spaghettini
THICK ROUND EGG NOODLES (wheat flour, egg, and water) *Danmian, cu*	FRESH: Boil for 2½ to 4 minutes DRIED: Boil for 7 to 9 minutes	soups, stir-fries	spaghetti, linguine
WHEAT-FLOUR NOODLES (flour and water) *Ganmian, biande*	FRESH: Boil for 2½ to 4 minutes DRIED: Boil for 4½ to 5 minutes	stir-fries, soups	linguine, fettuccine
RICE STICK NOODLES/ VERMICELLI (rice flour and water) *Mi fen*	Soften in hot water for 15 minutes, then boil or stir-fry for 45 seconds Deep-fry briefly in hot oil until lightly golden	soups, stir-fries deep-fried nests	somen, cellophane noodles

	NAME/INGREDIENTS	PREPARATION	USE	SUBSTITUTE
CHINESE NOODLES (cont.)	SPRING ROLL SKINS (wheat flour and water) *Chunjuan, pi*	Steam for 5 minutes	roll-ups, stir-fries	Mandarin pancakes, flour tortillas
		Deep-fry briefly in hot oil until golden brown and crisp	fried rolls	
	DUMPLING WRAPPERS (ROUND) (wheat flour and water) *Jiao, zi pi*	Boil, steam, or panfry FOR 5 TO 7 MINUTES	dumplings	wontons
		Deep-fry briefly in hot oil until golden brown and crisp		
	WONTON SKINS (SQUARE) (wheat flour, egg, and water) *Yundun, pi*	Boil for 3 to 4 minutes	wontons	dumpling wrappers
		Deep-fry briefly in hot oil until golden brown and crisp		
	CELLOPHANE NOODLES (mung bean starch and water) *Fensi*	Soften in hot water for 15 minutes, then boil or stir-fry for 1 minute	soups, stir-fries, salads	thin rice stick noodles
		Deep-fry briefly in hot oil until lightly golden	deep-fried nests	thin rice stick noodles

	NAME/INGREDIENTS	PREPARATION	USE	SUBSTITUTE
KOREAN NOODLES *Korean cooks also use Chinese rice sticks or thin egg noodles for stir-fries.*	SWEET POTATO VERMICELLI (sweet potato and mung bean starch) *Tangmyon*	Soften in hot water for 10 minutes, then stir-fry for 45 seconds to 1 minute	stir-fries	cellophane noodles, thin rice stick noodles
	BUCKWHEAT NOODLES (buckwheat flour and potato starch) *Naengmyon*	Boil for 3 to 3$\frac{1}{2}$ minutes	soups	soba, somen, thin rice stick noodles

JAPANESE NOODLES

Japanese cooks use an "add water" technique, letting the water reach a boil again after the noodles have been added, adding a cup of cold water, and letting it boil again, repeating this several times during cooking.

NAME/INGREDIENTS	PREPARATION	USE	SUBSTITUTE
SOBA NOODLES (buckwheat flour and water)	FRESH: Boil for 1 to 1½ minutes / DRIED: Boil for 4 to 4½ minutes	soups, stews, salads	udon
UDON NOODLES (wheat flour, egg, and water)	FRESH: Boil for 2 to 2½ minutes / DRIED: Boil for 10 to 12 minutes	soups, stews noodles	soba, Chinese wheat-flour
RAMEN NOODLES (wheat flour, egg, and water)	Boil for 4½ to 5 minutes	soups, stews, stir-fries	angel hair, thin Chinese egg noodles
SOMEN NOODLES (wheat flour and water)	Boil for 2½ to 3 minutes	soups, salads	soba, thin rice stick noodles, vermicelli

THAI NOODLES

Although rice noodles predominate, Thai cooks also use flat or thin Chinese egg noodles for stir-fries, and cellophane noodles for roll-ups and soups.

NAME/INGREDIENTS	PREPARATION	USE	SUBSTITUTE
THIN RICE STICKS/ VERMICELLI (rice flour and water) *Sen mee*	Soften in hot water for 15 minutes, then boil or stir-fry for 45 seconds	soups, stir-fries, salads	somen, angel hair, cellophane noodles
FLAT RICE STICKS/ VERMICELLI (THICK) (rice flour and water) *Sen yai*	Soften in hot water for 15 minutes, then boil or stir-fry for 45 seconds	soups, stir-fries, salads	thin rice stick noodles
JANTABOON (MEDIUM) *Sen lek*	Soften in hot water for 15 minutes, then boil or stir-fry for 45 seconds	stir-fries	thin rice stick noodles

**VIET-
NAMESE
NOODLES**

Vietnamese
cooks also
use flat or
thin Chinese
egg noodles
for stir-fries
and soups,
and cello-
phane noo-
dles for
soups and
roll-ups.

NAME/INGREDIENTS	PREPARATION	USE	SUBSTITUTE
THIN RICE STICKS/ VERMICELLI (rice flour and water) *Bun*	Soften in hot water 15 minutes, then boil or stir-fry for 45 seconds	roll-ups, salads, soups	somen, cellophane noodles
FLAT RICE STICKS/ VERMICELLI (rice flour and water) *Ban pho*	Soften in hot water 15 minutes, then boil or stir-fry for 45 seconds	soups (thin and medium), stir-fries (wide)	thin rice stick noodles
RICE PAPER WRAPPERS (rice flour and water)	Dip in hot water briefly to soften	fresh rolls	spring roll skins
	Deep-fry briefly in hot oil until golden brown and crisp	fried rolls	

Using the Recipes

❧ Read the ingredient list thoroughly, have all the ingredients at your fingertips, prepare all sauces, dips, marinades, blends, and pastes as instructed before proceeding with the recipe.

❧ All recipes are for six servings. To prepare two or three servings, divide the recipe in half.

❧ All the recipes use medium-grade, or all-purpose, soy sauce, unless otherwise specified. If substituting a "lite" soy or tamari, add the specified amount and season to taste.

❧ Like soy sauces, fish sauces vary in saltiness and flavor depending on the manufacturer. I tend to prefer the Thai version (*nam pla*), but the Vietnamese version (*nuoc mam*) is equally good.

❧ Toasted sesame oil, which is extracted from toasted sesame seeds, has a strong, pungent flavor. I prefer the Japanese brands, which are consistently good and are sold in supermarkets and specialty stores.

❧ Homemade chicken broth is recommended for preparing any soup (see the Chinese Chicken Broth recipe, page 53), but for most recipes a good-quality low-sodium canned broth can be used. You can doctor the flavor by adding some rice wine or sake and several slices of smashed ginger, then simmer for 5 to 8 minutes. Remove the ginger and reserve for another use.

❧ The end of a chopstick, or a scallion tip, can be used to test the temperature of oil when frying food. Look for the following signs: At 350°F, the bubbles merging from the tip are quite small and make no sound. At 375°F, the bubbles are bigger, they appear more rapidly, and there is a slight sizzling noise. The correct temperature for frying depends on the food to be cooked.

❧ To create an attractive, flowerlike shape, shrimp are often scored. Lay the shrimp on a work surface and, using a sharp knife, make a shallow cut down the back starting at the head and stopping just short of the tail. Then remove the vein. When the shrimp is exposed to heat it will curl.

❧ Noodles symbolize longevity and Asians like them long. Westerners may not be quite as comfortable with long noodles, and for many dishes, I clip my cooked, rinsed noodles into 3-inch lengths with kitchen shears before serving.

❧ Asians, unlike Westerners, like to rinse their cooked noodles to remove excess starch. For colder room-temperature noodle dishes, rinse in warmer water; for salads, rinse cooked noodles in cold.

15

Boiled Noodles

THE SECRET TO EVENLY COOKED NOODLES is the amount of water you cook them in. Boil enough water so that the noodles will have plenty of room to move around. I like to slightly undercook them, so they are just tender, or *al dente*, and it is also advisable to rinse them once they have been cooked to remove the excess starch. Check pages 10–13 for specific cooking times.

I pound fresh or dried noodles

1. In a large pot, bring 4 quarts of water to a rolling boil. Add the noodles and gently separate by stirring them with chopsticks or a wooden spoon. When the water returns to a boil, reduce heat to medium high and cook, stirring occasionally, until the noodles are tender but firm.
2. Drain the noodles in a colander, rinse under cold or warm water as directed, and drain again. (If you overcook the noodles, immediately refresh them in cold water to firm them up.)
Note: To reheat noodles for soups, bring 3 quarts of water to a boil in a large pot. Place the cooked noodles in a colander with a handle and set it in the water so that the noodles are completely immersed. Boil, stirring, for 20 seconds and drain thoroughly. Alternatively, place the cooked noodles in a colander in the sink and pour boiling water over them. Drain thoroughly.

6 SERVINGS

basic recipe

Noodle Starters and Sides

IN ASIA, LIGHT NOODLE DISHES ARE ROUTINELY SERVED as starter courses. In Japan, at both elegant and funky noodle houses all over Tokyo specializing in soba, noodles are often the first course: Mounds of them are arranged on sleek bamboo mats and accompanied by a pungent wasabi dipping sauce. The noodles are intriguing in their simplicity. They are delicious—light and clean-tasting—and such an enticing way to begin the meal.

In China, cold noodle salads are traditionally offered at the beginning of sumptuous banquets. Layers of sliced meat, seafood, and fresh vegetables are arranged on platters of noodles, sometimes in colorful mosaic patterns. One of the most memorable is spicy sesame noodles, where shredded chicken and cucumbers are drizzled with a spicy toasted sesame dressing perfumed with garlic, ginger, and hot peppers. Soaked in the velvety dressing, the noodles are slippery and sensual.

In Vietnam and Thailand, noodle starters take the form of roll-ups: Assorted stir-fried mixtures are lightly dressed, tossed with boiled or crisp-fried noodles, and scooped up in lettuce leaves or moistened rice noodle wrappers. Vietnamese spring rolls are typically filled with pork barbecued in a honey glaze, shrimp, carrots, lettuce, and rice vermicelli noodles with fresh mint and cilantro. These are casual finger foods, which convey a lively sense of spontaneity.

Asian noodle dishes are ideal first courses because they incorporate many familiar ingredients in unexpected ways. They are especially suited to the busy cook, since most require almost effortless, impromptu preparation.

I'm always inspired by the classic dishes to create new variations. I

21

grill all types of seafood and meat, arrange them over briefly cooked fresh vegetables, and drizzle the platters with spicy dressings. I mix and match ingredients with contrasting textures and tastes—tender, sweet scallops with crisp broccoli and red bell peppers as in Ginger Scallops with Thin Noodles, smooth noodles with crunchy vegetable toppings, and spicy hot chiles with sweet-and-sour dressings. I usually use lighter noodles, such as thin rice vermicelli, cellophane noodles, and angel hair pasta, so the dishes won't be too filling.

Noodle side dishes, on the other hand, are for the most part delicately flavored so that they don't upstage the main course. Stir-fried Ginger-Scallion Noodles go beautifully with cooked seafood of any kind. Fiery Chile Noodles are seasoned a bit more assertively and are best served with heartier dishes, such as grilled or roasted meat.

Like the starters, noodle side dishes lend themselves to improvisation and variety. In the fall, when wild mushrooms are abundant, I toss them with leeks and rice noodles and serve them with roast meat. In the summer, I like to cook festive, colorful noodles with strips of zucchini and yellow squash, doused with a fresh cilantro dressing. Some noodle side dishes are more substantial, with different mixes of meat, seafood, and vegetables. One of my favorites, Curried Vegetarian Noodles, a colorful blend of shredded onions, red bell peppers, and Napa cabbage, is so satisfying I don't hesitate to serve it as a simple meal by itself.

Vietnamese Spring Rolls

THESE DELICATE ROLLS ARE PERFECT PORTABLE little noodle salads. They are great for entertaining. Simply prepare them several hours in advance and cover with plastic wrap to keep them moist. You can add barbecued pork (as in the classic recipe) or substitute other cooked meat or seafood.

1. Preheat the oven to 375°F. Put the pork in an aluminum foil–lined baking pan, add the garlicky marinade, and turn to coat. Roast about 35 minutes, or until the pork is cooked through. Let cool, then cut into thin 1¹/₂-inch-long slices.

2. In a large bowl, toss together the pork, rice noodles, carrots, mint, and cilantro.

3. Fill a wide shallow pan with hot water and spread a dish towel out on a work surface. Dip a rice wrapper into the warm water for about 3 seconds, until softened, and place it in front of you on the towel.

4. Place a lettuce leaf on the lower third of the rice wrapper. Arrange 2 tablespoons of the noodle mixture on the lettuce. Fold the bottom edge over the filling, tucking in the sides. Place 2 shrimp halves, cut side down, and roll up into a tight cylinder. Place the roll on a platter and cover with a damp towel to prevent it from drying out. Repeat with the remaining wrappers, filling, and shrimp. Serve with the sweet-and-sour sauce and spicy peanut sauce.

MAKES 35 ROLLS

1 pound pork tenderloin, trimmed of fat and gristle

Garlicky Marinade **Blend together**
3 tablespoons soy sauce
1¹/₂ tablespoons minced garlic
1¹/₂ tablespoons honey

¹/₂ pound thin rice stick noodles (vermicelli), softened in hot water, cooked until just tender, rinsed under cold water, and drained
2 large carrots, peeled and shredded or grated
³/₄ cup fresh mint leaves, coarsely shredded
³/₄ cup fresh cilantro leaves, coarsely shredded

35 round rice paper wrappers (about 8 inches in diameter)
2 heads Boston lettuce, leaves separated, rinsed, dried, and the tough center ribs trimmed
1¹/₂ pounds medium shrimp, poached in boiling water until pink, peeled, sliced in half lengthwise, and deveined
Spicy Sweet-and-Sour Dipping Sauce (page 117) and Peanut Sauce (page 116) for dipping

23

Cold Soba Noodles

SOBA NOODLES CAN EASILY BECOME ADDICTIVE, especially if chilled and served with a fiery wasabi dipping sauce. The contrast of hot and cold is incredibly appealing. Don't forget to slurp them noisily, as the Japanese do, to show your enjoyment.

2 tablespoons wasabi powder

6 tablespoons finely chopped scallion greens

Dipping Sauce **Mix together and chill**

2 cups Japanese Broth (page 54)

$^{1}/_{4}$ cup soy sauce

3 tablespoons mirin (sweetened rice wine)

$^{3}/_{4}$ **pound soba, cooked until just tender, rinsed under cold water, drained, and chilled**

1. Mix the wasabi with $3^{1}/_{2}$ tablespoons of water to form a paste, then divide evenly among six small plates. Place 1 tablespoon scallions on each plate. Divide the dipping sauce among six small bowls. Divide the noodles evenly among six serving bowls.

2. To eat the noodles, mix a dab of the wasabi and some scallions with the dipping sauce, then dip some of the noodles into the sauce.

6 SERVINGS

24

Garlic Soba with Broccoli Rabe

I FIRST FELL IN LOVE WITH SOBA in the little noodle houses in Japan. There the noodles are served hot in soups or cold with a fiery horseradish dressing. I stir-fry them with all kinds of vegetables and light sauces. In this recipe, they're simply tossed with lots of garlic, crisp-cooked broccoli rabe, and toasted pine nuts. Substitute broccoli or cauliflower if you can't find broccoli rabe.

1½ tablespoons safflower or corn oil

1½ teaspoons toasted sesame oil

2 tablespoons very thinly sliced garlic

1½ teaspoons crushed red pepper

1½ pounds broccoli rabe, trimmed, leafy tips discarded, and cut on the diagonal into 1-inch lengths

¼ cup Chinese rice wine or sake, mixed with 3 tablespoons water

1 pound soba, cooked until just tender, rinsed under warm water, and drained

Sweet Soy Sauce **Mix together**

3 tablespoons soy sauce

2 tablespoons water

1½ teaspoons sugar

¾ cup toasted pine nuts (optional)

1. Heat a wok or a heavy skillet over medium heat. Add both the oils and heat until hot, about 30 seconds. Add the garlic and red pepper and stir-fry until the garlic is lightly golden, about 30 seconds. Add the broccoli rabe, turn up the heat to high, and add the rice wine mixture. Stir-fry for 30 seconds, then cover and cook for 1½ to 2 minutes, or until the broccoli is tender.

2. Add the noodles, sweet soy sauce mix, and pine nuts, if using, and stir-fry to blend. Transfer to a serving bowl and serve.

6 SERVINGS

Chile Noodles

I SERVE STIR-FRIED CHILE NOODLES THROUGHOUT THE SUMMER with grilled meat and seafood. The hot-and-sour dressing seems to taste especially delicious then. Sometimes I use multicolored peppers, eggplant, or green beans in place of the zucchini and squash.

1 1/2 tablespoons safflower or corn oil

2 1/2 tablespoons toasted sesame oil

1 1/2 teaspoons crushed red pepper

2 1/2 tablespoons minced fresh ginger

2 tablespoons minced garlic

1 large red onion, thinly sliced into 1 1/2-inch-long strips

3 medium zucchini, cut into thin 1 1/2-inch-long strips

3 medium yellow squash, cut into 1 1/2-inch-long strips

Rice Wine Dressing Mix together

1/2 cup soy sauce

3 1/2 tablespoons Chinese rice wine or sake

2 1/2 tablespoons sugar

3 tablespoons Chinese black vinegar or Worcestershire sauce

1 pound soba or flat spinach noodles, such as fettuccine, cooked until just tender, rinsed under warm water, and drained

1/4 cup minced fresh parsley

1. Heat a wok or a heavy skillet over high heat. Add both the oils and heat until hot, about 30 seconds. Add the red pepper, ginger, and garlic and stir-fry until fragrant, about 15 seconds. Add the onion and stir-fry until slightly limp, about 1 minute. Add the zucchini and yellow squash and stir-fry until barely tender, about 1 1/2 minutes.

2. Add the rice wine dressing and the noodles and toss lightly to coat the ingredients with the dressing. Add the parsley and toss lightly. Transfer to a serving platter and serve.

6 SERVINGS

Ginger-Scallion Noodles

I FIRST TASTED THIS DISH AT ONE OF my favorite Cantonese restaurants in Boston. I like to order it with garlicky dishes such as clams in black bean sauce and lobster Cantonese. At home, I serve it with grilled seafood or meat, but the vibrant scallion-ginger seasonings are so subtle you can serve it with almost any entrée.

1½ tablespoons safflower or corn oil

3 cups finely shredded scallions

¾ cup finely shredded fresh ginger

⅓ cup Chinese rice wine or sake

3 cups bean sprouts, rinsed and drained

Sesame Sauce **Mix together**

½ cup Chinese Chicken Broth (page 53)

1½ tablespoons toasted sesame oil

1½ teaspoons salt, or to taste

½ teaspoon freshly ground black pepper

1 teaspoon cornstarch

½ pound thin **Chinese** egg noodles or angel hair, cooked until just tender, rinsed under cold water, and drained

1. Heat a wok or a heavy skillet over high heat. Add the oil and heat until very hot but not smoking, about 30 seconds. Add the scallions and ginger and stir-fry until fragrant, about 20 seconds. Add the rice wine and bean sprouts and toss lightly for about 1 minute.

2. Add the sesame sauce and the noodles and stir-fry until the sauce thickens, about 2 minutes. Transfer to a platter and serve.

6 SERVINGS

Cilantro Noodles

CILANTRO HAS A FRESH, SLIGHTLY MUSKY FLAVOR that people either love or hate. I've come to adore it. In this dish, it intensifies the sweetness of the carrots and leeks, creating a delicious contrast to the tangy vinaigrette. Serve these noodles with grilled seafood or chicken.

1. Heat a wok or a heavy skillet over high heat. Add both the oils and heat until hot, about 30 seconds. Add the leek and ginger and stir-fry for about 1 1/2 minutes, until the leeks are slightly limp. Add the carrots and rice wine and stir-fry for about 1 1/2 minutes, until the carrots are just tender. Add the bean sprouts and toss lightly for 1 minute.

2. Add the noodles, the tangy soy dressing, and the cilantro and toss lightly until heated through. Transfer to a serving bowl and serve.

6 SERVINGS

2 tablespoons toasted sesame oil

1 tablespoon safflower or corn oil

3 cups finely shredded leeks (cut into 1 1/2-inch-long shreds)

2 tablespoons minced fresh ginger

3 medium carrots, shredded or grated (2 cups)

3 tablespoons Chinese rice wine or sake

3 cups bean sprouts, rinsed and drained

1/2 pound thin rice stick noodles (vermicelli), softened in hot water, cooked until just tender, rinsed under cold water, and drained

Tangy Soy Dressing Mix together

7 tablespoons soy sauce

2 tablespoons sugar

3 tablespoons Japanese rice vinegar

1/2 cup chopped fresh cilantro

31

Wild Mushroom Noodles

SUPERMARKET PRODUCE COUNTERS ARE NOW A HAVEN for wild mushroom lovers like me. There are shiitakes, creminis, meaty portobellos, and more. I use whatever varieties are available and toss them in with generous amounts of garlic and nutty soba noodles to make a simple side dish that's superb with roasted meat.

1 tablespoon safflower or corn oil

12 cloves garlic, mashed with the flat side of a knife and very thinly sliced

8 dried Chinese black mushrooms, softened in hot water, drained, stems removed, and caps thinly sliced

1/2 pound shiitake mushrooms, rinsed, drained, stem ends trimmed, and caps thinly sliced

1/2 pound cremini mushrooms, rinsed, drained, stems trimmed, and caps thinly sliced

3 1/2 tablespoons Chinese rice wine or sake

1 1/2 cups minced scallion greens

3/4 pound soba or thin noodles, such as spaghettini, cooked until just tender, rinsed under warm water, and drained

3 1/2 tablespoons soy sauce

1/4 cup chopped fresh cilantro

1. Heat a wok or a heavy skillet over high heat. Add the oil and heat until hot, about 30 seconds. Add the garlic and black mushrooms and stir-fry until fragrant, about 15 seconds.

2. Add the fresh mushrooms and stir-fry for 1 to 2 minutes, until slightly softened. Lower the heat to medium high and add the rice wine. Partially cover and cook for about 3 1/2 minutes, or until the mushrooms are tender. Uncover, add the scallions, and cook to reduce the liquid by half.

3. Add the noodles and the soy sauce and stir-fry briefly to mix. Add the cilantro and toss to mix. Transfer to a platter and serve.

6 SERVINGS

Curried Vegetarian Noodles

SINGAPORE IS A HAVEN FOR LOVERS OF NOODLES OF ALL KINDS, since every ethnic variety is available there. You can eat noodles from dawn to dusk from the thousands of food stalls strewn about the city. I first tasted a version of this dish in a hole-in-the-wall shop in one of the city's foremost hawkers' centers. It was studded with shrimp and barbecued pork. Inspired by the superb mix of flavors, I created this vegetarian version with red onions, bell peppers, and Chinese cabbage, all lightly dusted with curry powder and seasoned generously with garlic and ginger.

1½ tablespoons safflower or corn oil

Curry Seasonings Mix together
1½ tablespoons minced garlic
1 tablespoon minced fresh ginger
1½ tablespoons curry powder, preferably Madras

2½ cups very thinly sliced red onions
2 cups thinly sliced red bell peppers
4 cups thinly sliced Napa cabbage

Basic Chinese Sauce Mix together
¼ cup **Chinese Chicken Broth (page 53)**
3 tablespoons soy sauce
½ teaspoon sugar
1 teaspoon salt
¼ teaspoon freshly ground black pepper

½ pound thin rice stick noodles (vermicelli), softened in hot water and drained

1. Heat a wok or a heavy skillet over high heat. Add the oil and heat until very hot, about 30 seconds. Add the curry seasonings and stir-fry until fragrant, about 10 seconds. Add the red onions and stir-fry for about 1 minute, until barely tender. Add the red peppers and stir-fry for 1 minute, then add the cabbage and cook for 2 to 3 minutes, until all are crisp-tender.
2. Add the basic Chinese sauce and the noodles, and carefully toss to mix. Cook, stirring, for 30 seconds. Transfer to a serving dish and serve hot or at room temperature.

6 SERVINGS

34

Ginger Scallops with Thin Noodles

PLUMP CHAR-GRILLED SCALLOPS, RED BELL PEPPERS, and crisp-tender broccoli seasoned with a lively ginger teriyaki sauce top the noodles in this appetizer. When I feel extravagant, I use lobster meat and snow peas.

Ginger Marinade
6 tablespoons soy sauce
6 tablespoons water
$^1/_3$ cup Chinese rice wine or sake
$4^1/_2$ tablespoons sugar
$1^1/_2$ tablespoons minced fresh ginger
$^1/_2$ teaspoon crushed red pepper (optional)
$1^1/_2$ tablespoons cornstarch

$1^1/_2$ pounds sea scallops, rinsed and drained

1 pound broccoli, stalks and florets separated, stalks peeled and cut on the diagonal into $1^1/_2$-inch lengths
1 tablespoon safflower or corn oil
2 red bell peppers, cored, seeded, and thinly sliced

$^1/_2$ pound thin noodles, such as angel hair, cooked until just tender, rinsed under cold water, and drained

Ten 10-inch bamboo skewers (soaked in water for 1 hour) or metal skewers

1. Combine the marinade ingredients over medium heat, stirring constantly to prevent lumps, until thickened, 1 to 2 minutes. Remove and cool.
2. Combine half the marinade and scallops; toss lightly to coat. Let sit 1 hour at room temperature or cover to refrigerate overnight.
3. Add the broccoli to a large pot of boiling water; cook 3 minutes, or until crisp-tender. Drain, refresh in cold water, and drain again.
4. Prepare a grill or preheat the broiler.
5. Thread the scallops on the skewers; keep the marinade. Place the scallops about 3 inches from the heat source and cook about 3 minutes. Turn, brush with scallop marinade, and cook 3 minutes longer, or until golden. Transfer to a plate and cover to keep warm.
6. Heat a wok or a heavy skillet over high heat. Add the oil and heat until very hot but not smoking. Add the red peppers and toss lightly for 1 minute, or until just tender. Add the broccoli, the set aside half of the marinade, and the noodles and toss to mix. Transfer to a platter, arrange the scallops on top, and serve.

6 SERVINGS

Crispy Shrimp Balls

THESE WHIMSICAL APPETIZERS, OR HORS D'OEUVRES, are inspired by hundred-corner shrimp balls, a traditional Shanghai dim sum dish. Instead of bread crumbs, I use rice stick noodles to make the delightfully crisp coating.

²/₃ **pound medium shrimp, peeled, scored down the back, deveined, rinsed, and patted dry**

¹/₂ **cup water chestnuts, blanched in boiling water for 10 seconds, refreshed in cold water, drained, and patted dry**

Shrimp Ball Seasonings
1¹/₂ **tablespoons minced fresh ginger**
1¹/₂ **tablespoons minced scallions**
1¹/₂ **tablespoons Chinese rice wine or sake**
1 **teaspoon toasted sesame oil**
³/₄ **teaspoon salt**

1 **large egg white, lightly beaten**
2 **tablespoons cornstarch**
¹/₄ **pound thin rice stick noodles (vermicelli)**
Safflower or corn oil for deep-frying

Plum or duck sauce and hot mustard for dipping

1. In a food processor fitted with a steel blade, process the shrimp to a paste. Transfer to a large bowl; add the water chestnuts, seasonings, egg white, and cornstarch. Stir vigorously until a stiff paste forms. Chill thoroughly.

2. With a towel draped over the hand that holds a sharp knife, cut the noodles into ¹/₂-inch lengths. The towel prevents the noodles from flying around. Spread evenly on a cookie sheet.

3. Shape scant teaspoonfuls of the shrimp mixture into balls, then roll in the noodle pieces, pressing lightly to coat. Set on a cookie sheet.

4. Heat a wok or a deep skillet or saucepan over high. Add the oil and heat to 375°F. Deep-fry the shrimp balls in batches, turning them constantly, until golden brown, 3 to 4 minutes. Remove with a handled strainer or a slotted spoon, drain briefly in a colander, then transfer to paper towels. Between batches, skim the oil with a fine strainer, and reheat until hot. Serve the shrimp balls warm with sauce and mustard. To reheat, warm on a cookie sheet in a 375°F oven about 10 minutes.

MAKES 30 TO 32 BALLS

38

Fresh Shrimp Rolls

THESE ARE MY VERSION OF VIETNAMESE SPRING ROLLS, which are traditionally made with both pork and shrimp. Light, fresh, and—best of all—transportable, they are, to my mind, more satisfying than the fried version.

6 ounces thin rice stick noodles (vermicelli), softened in hot water, cooked until just tender, rinsed under cold water and drained, and cut into 3-inch lengths

2 large carrots, peeled and grated

3/4 cup fresh Thai holy basil or sweet basil leaves, finely shredded

1/3 cup fresh cilantro leaves, coarsely chopped

Spicy Lime Dressing Mix together

3 tablespoons fish sauce

Juice of 2 limes

1 to 2 small jalapeño peppers, seeded and chopped

2 1/2 tablespoons sugar

24 round rice paper wrappers (about 8 inches in diameter)

1 to 2 heads Boston lettuce or 1 large head leaf lettuce, leaves separated, rinsed, and dried, and tough center ribs trimmed

1 pound medium shrimp, poached in boiling water until pink, peeled, sliced in half lengthwise, and deveined

Spicy Sweet-and-Sour Dipping Sauce (page 117) or Peanut Sauce (page 116) for dipping

1. In a bowl, combine the noodles, carrots, basil, and cilantro. Add the spicy lime dressing and toss lightly to coat.

2. Fill a wide shallow pan with hot water and spread a dish towel out on a work surface. Dip a rice wrapper in the water for about 3 seconds until softened and place on the towel.

3. Place a lettuce leaf on the lower third of the rice wrapper. Spoon a scant 1/4 cup of the noodle mixture onto the lettuce, arrange 2 shrimp halves next to each other, and roll up into a cylinder, tucking in the ends as you go. Place the roll on a platter and cover with a damp towel to prevent it from drying out. Repeat with remaining rice wrappers, noodles, and shrimp. Serve with the sweet-and-sour sauce or peanut sauce for dipping.

MAKES 24 ROLLS

Spicy Sesame Noodles

TOASTED SESAME PASTE IS THE CREAMY BASE for the spunky sauce here. Drizzled over smooth flat noodles and a spray of crisp vegetables, it transforms them into a luscious appetizer, perfect for a picnic basket. For a sumptuous vegetarian salad, leave out the chicken and add more vegetables.

I pound flat **Chinese** egg noodles or other flat noodles, such as fettuccine or linguine, cooked until just tender, rinsed under cold water, drained, and tossed with I teaspoon toasted sesame oil

2 English (seedless) cucumbers, peeled, halved lengthwise, seeded, and grated

I red bell pepper, cored, seeded, and thinly sliced

I 1/2 cups bean sprouts, rinsed and drained

I 1/2 cups sliced cooked chicken (cut into thin strips)

3 tablespoons minced scallion greens

2 tablespoons toasted sesame seeds (optional)

Spicy Sesame Dressing (page 120)

1. Arrange the noodles on a large deep platter.
2. Scatter the cucumbers, red pepper, and bean sprouts over the noodles, leaving a shallow well in the center for the chicken. Arrange the chicken in the center. Sprinkle with the scallion greens and sesame seeds.
3. Serve with the spicy sesame dressing on the side.

6 SERVINGS

Chicken Noodle Satay

THE CREAMY PEANUT–COCONUT MILK SAUCE traditionally served with satay is a superb dressing for fresh vegetables and seared meats. It takes only minutes to prepare in the food processor. I keep a vat in my refrigerator (it will last for two weeks) for instant use. The delicate rice stick vermicelli noodles give the dish substance yet keep it appealingly light.

Satay Marinade

$1/4$ **cup fish sauce**

2 tablespoons minced fresh lemongrass

I tablespoon minced garlic

$1^1/2$ **pounds boneless, skinless chicken breasts, cut into $1/6$-inch-thick slices**

$3/4$ **pound thin rice stick noodles (vermicelli), softened in hot water, cooked until just tender, rinsed under cold water, and drained**

5 carrots, peeled and finely shredded or grated

$2^1/2$ **cups thinly sliced Boston lettuce leaves**

$1^1/2$ **cups bean sprouts, rinsed and drained**

About I tablespoon safflower or corn oil

3 tablespoons minced fresh cilantro

Satay Sauce (page I 17)

1. In a medium bowl, combine the satay marinade ingredients. Add the chicken and toss lightly to coat. Cover with plastic wrap and let marinate for at least 2 hours or overnight in the refrigerator.

2. Arrange the noodles on a serving platter and top with the carrots, lettuce, and bean sprouts, arranging them randomly or in separate concentric circles and reserving room in the center for the chicken.

3. Heat a heavy skillet over high heat. Add 1 teaspoon oil and heat until almost smoking hot. Add the chicken in batches and sear for about $1^1/2$ minutes, until firm to the touch and golden brown on both sides, adding more oil to the pan as needed. Arrange the chicken over the noodles and sprinkle the cilantro on top. Pass the satay sauce separately.

6 SERVINGS

Curried Chicken Rolls

IF YOUR CURRY POWDER USUALLY COMES from the spice section of the super-market, this home-ground version will change your mind forever. Curry powder can be made with up to twenty spices, but mine is a simple combination of some of the most pungent seasonings.

24 spring roll skins or flour tortillas

3 tablespoons safflower or corn oil

2 leeks, trimmed, thoroughly cleaned, and cut into thin 1¹/₂-inch-long strips

5 carrots, peeled and grated

2 turnips, peeled and grated

2¹/₂ tablespoons Chinese rice wine or sake

Home-ground Curry Powder Chop to a paste in a food processor

¹/₂ teaspoon crushed red pepper

8 cloves garlic, peeled

One 2¹/₂-inch piece ginger, cut into 4 or 5 slices

1¹/₂ teaspoons ground cumin

1 teaspoon ground coriander

¹/₂ teaspoon ground turmeric

1 teaspoon salt

¹/₂ teaspoon freshly ground black pepper

1 pound boneless, skinless chicken breasts, cut into ¹/₆-inch-thick slices

Coconut Sauce Blend together

1 cup coconut milk

2 tablespoons fish sauce

1 tablespoon sugar

1 cup fresh sweet basil leaves, coarsely chopped

1. Separate the spring roll skins and fold in half or quarters. Arrange in a steamer and steam for 5 minutes. Set aside.

2. Heat a wok or a heavy skillet over medium-high heat. Add 1¹/₂ tablespoons of the oil and heat about 30 seconds. Add the leeks and stir-fry for 1 minute, or until they soften. Add the carrots, turnips, and rice wine, and toss lightly. Cover, turn the heat down to medium, and cook for 2 minutes, or until the carrots and turnips are tender. Transfer the vegetables to a bowl and set aside.

3. Reheat the wok, add the remaining 1¹/₂ tablespoons oil, and heat until hot, about 30 seconds. Add the home-ground curry powder and cook for 20 seconds, or until very fragrant. Add the chicken, turn up the heat to high, and stir-fry until the meat loses its pink color and the slices separate. Add the coconut sauce and cook for about 10 minutes, or until it thickens. Add the leek mixture and chopped basil, toss lightly, and transfer to a platter. To eat, spoon some of the curry mixture onto a wrapper and roll up.

6 SERVINGS

46

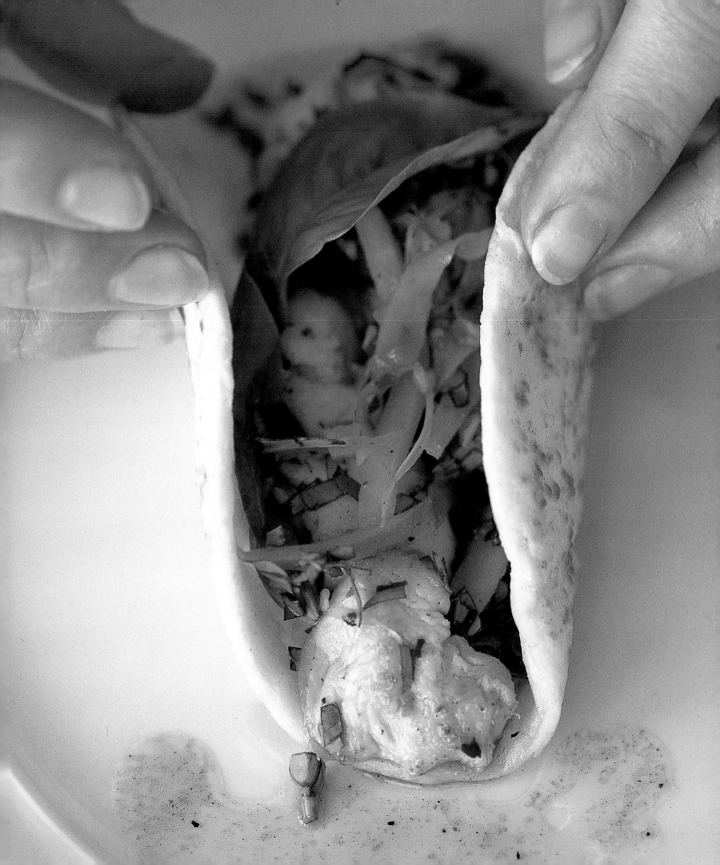

Spicy Korean Beef Noodles

I CRAVE SPICY SEASONINGS LIKE GARLIC, ginger, and hot chiles. And I love to counterbalance the heat with fresh vegetables such as the lettuce wrappers in this dish. The crisp fried rice stick noodles add yet another textural contrast to the tender cooked beef.

2 heads Boston lettuce, leaves separated, rinsed, and dried

2 ounces thin rice stick noodles, deep-fried as directed on page 10

Korean Seasonings

3 1/2 tablespoons minced scallions (white part only)

1 1/2 tablespoons minced fresh ginger

1 tablespoon minced garlic

1 1/2 teaspoons toasted sesame oil

1/2 pound lean ground beef

1 1/2 teaspoons safflower or corn oil

Spicy Sauce **Mix together**

5 tablespoons Chinese ground bean sauce or sweet bean paste

1/4 cup sugar

2 tablespoons toasted sesame oil

1 1/2 teaspoons hot chile paste

1 pound firm tofu, wrapped in paper towels and weighted for 30 minutes, then cut into 1/4-inch cubes

1. Trim any tough center ribs from the lettuce leaves and press them gently to flatten them. Arrange in a basket or a serving bowl. Arrange the fried noodles on a serving platter, crumbling them gently to break them up.

2. In a medium bowl, combine the Korean seasonings. Add the beef and mix well.

3. Heat a wok or heavy skillet over medium-high heat. Add the oil and heat until hot, about 30 seconds. Add the meat and stir-fry, breaking up any lumps, until it loses its pink color. Drain in a colander and wipe out the wok.

4. Reheat the wok, add the spicy sauce, cooking and stirring until it reduces and thickens, 3 to 4 minutes. Add the tofu and beef and toss to coat. Spoon the mixture over the fried noodles. To eat, spoon about 1 1/2 tablespoons of the noodle mixture onto a lettuce leaf and roll it up, tucking in the sides.

6 SERVINGS

Noodle Soups

THERE IS NO DISH MORE COMFORTING OR SUSTAINING than a bowl of noodle soup. It's the ultimate "Mommy food" in any country. Asian noodle soups not only nurture—every spoonful offers a different and exciting flavor experience. Try the Vietnamese Hot-and-Sour Shrimp Soup: A subtle broth is complemented by a masterful interplay of contrasting hot, sweet, and sour tastes. Lemongrass, lime juice, and crushed red pepper add a mouth-tingling element to shrimp, mushrooms, and bean sprouts. Hanoi Beef Noodles, or *pho*, the quintessential Vietnamese dish, is no less exciting with its intense anise-and-cinnamon-flavored broth, tender pieces of braised beef, crisp bean sprouts, and smooth rice noodles. Scallions and fresh herbs—cilantro and basil—sprinkled on at the last moment add a delightful freshness.

Japanese soups, with their smoky broth, or *dashi*, are equally spectacular. Some are garnished with vibrantly colored toppings of shrimp, scallops, and assorted vegetables. Others are simple robust meat and noodle pots, one-dish meals served in casseroles, like Mushroom-Beef Udon Soup with its zaftig wheat-flour noodles floating amid slices of sirloin and both dried and fresh shiitake mushrooms. Scallion Chicken with Soba Soup is also simple but totally satisfying.

Chinese and Thai soups are equally varied. One of my Chinese favorites, hearty Cinnamon Beef Noodles, features tender braised meat and a rich broth suffused with the flavor of cinnamon, aniseed, and soy sauce. Another Chinese classic offers poached shrimp and tender tendrils of pea shoots in a delicate broth. One of the most basic but soulful soups pre-

51

pared by Thai cooks highlights hard-shell clams, cooked in their own juices with a touch of rice wine and handfuls of fresh basil thrown in to finish. It's quick, easy, and endlessly satisfying.

With any soup, the crucial factor is a sound base or broth. Making stock is easy—it merely requires some cooking time. Chicken or beef broths are the most versatile; seasonings such as fresh ginger, scallions, cinnamon sticks, and rice wine add further dimension.

Of course, the noodle must fit the dish. I use delicate, ethereal noodles such as cellophane, rice vermicelli, and somen in light, refined soups. Buckwheat and medium-size wheat-flour-and-egg noodles are reserved for more substantial broths. And thick round or flat wheat-flour and rice-flour strands stand up to hearty stews and casseroles.

Perhaps one of the most appealing qualities of Asian soups is that most can be prepared quickly, with a minimum of fuss, and yet provide infinite pleasure.

Chinese Chicken Broth

GOOD SOUP STARTS WITH A GOOD BASE. Mine is pretty straightforward—chicken bones, rice wine, and fresh ginger. I like to make a large batch, and freeze it in small quantities. It will keep in the refrigerator up to a week and in ice cube trays to use cube by cube for sauces.

1. Combine the chicken bones, water, rice wine, and ginger in a large pot and bring to a boil. Reduce the heat to low and simmer, uncovered, for 1 1/2 hours, skimming the surface to remove any foam or impurities.

2. Strain the broth through a fine strainer into a bowl or another pot. Skim to remove any fat. (Alternatively, cool and refrigerate the broth and then remove the solidified fat.)

MAKES ABOUT 6 CUPS

3 1/2 pounds chicken bones, necks, backs, and/or pieces

9 cups water

I cup **Chinese rice wine or sake**

6 slices **fresh ginger (about the size of a quarter), lightly smashed with the flat side of a knife**

53

Japanese Broth (Dashi)

DASHI IS THE BASE FOR MOST JAPANESE SOUPS. The flavor is subtle and enticingly smoky, and it takes only minutes to prepare. Kelp and bonito shavings can be found in most health food stores as well as Asian markets. The dashi will keep up to a week in the refrigerator. I don't recommend freezing this broth—and there's really no need to since it is so easy to make.

One 4-inch square giant kelp (konbu), cleaned with a damp cloth

4 cups cold water

2/3 cup dried bonito flakes (katsuo-bushi)

1. Combine the kelp and water in a large pot and bring it to a boil. Immediately remove the kelp with tongs. (Reserve it for another use.)
2. Add the bonito flakes, stir well, and remove from the heat. Let the flakes settle to the bottom of the pot (about 1 minute), then strain through a fine strainer (or a coarse strainer lined with cheesecloth).

MAKES ABOUT 4 CUPS

54

Vietnamese Hot-and-Sour Shrimp Soup

EVERY TIME I MAKE THIS SOUP, I marvel at the intriguing blend of seasonings, with the contrasts among the crushed red pepper, the fresh lemongrass, and the tart lime juice. A bonus is that it can be prepared quickly and served immediately—just like a bowl of instant soup. You simply add water rather than preparing a stock.

1. Heat a heavy pot or casserole over medium-high heat. Add the oil and heat until hot, about 30 seconds. Add the shallots and lemongrass and stir-fry for about 15 seconds. Add the tomato, mushrooms, and sugar and stir-fry for about 1 minute. Add the water and bring to a boil. Reduce the heat to medium and simmer, uncovered, for about 10 minutes.

2. Add the shrimp, fish sauce, lime juice, and noodles and simmer for about 2 minutes, or until the shrimp turn pink and the noodles are tender. Using tongs, remove and discard the lemongrass. Add the bean sprouts and crushed red pepper, bring to a boil, and cook for about 1 minute, or until heated through. Ladle into soup bowls, sprinkle with the scallions, and serve.

6 SERVINGS

1 teaspoon safflower or corn oil

2 tablespoons minced shallots

2 stalks lemongrass, trimmed, wilted or tough outer leaves discarded, cut into 2-inch lengths, and smashed lightly with the flat side of a knife

1 large ripe tomato, cored, seeded, and cut into 1/4-inch-thick wedges

1/2 pound button mushrooms, rinsed, drained, stems trimmed, and caps thinly sliced

1 1/2 teaspoons sugar

5 cups water

1/2 pound medium shrimp, peeled, scored down the back, deveined, and rinsed

5 1/2 tablespoons fish sauce

3 tablespoons fresh lime juice

1/4 pound very thin rice stick noodles (vermicelli), softened in hot water and drained

1 1/2 cups bean sprouts, rinsed and drained

1/2 teaspoon crushed red pepper

2 tablespoons finely minced scallion greens

Shrimp and Pea Shoot Soup

THIS IS THE QUINTESSENTIAL CHINESE SOUP—an extra-light, fresh, and refined broth, brimming with barely poached seafood. Pea shoots are the delicate leafy tendrils of snow pea vines. They're sold in Asian markets and specialty food shops. If pea shoots aren't available, substitute snow peas or snap peas.

5¹/₂ ounces somen or other very thin noodles, such as angel hair, cooked until just tender, rinsed under warm water, and drained

1 pound medium shrimp, peeled, scored down the back, deveined, and rinsed

2 tablespoons Chinese rice wine or sake

2 teaspoons minced fresh ginger

1 teaspoon safflower or corn oil

1 tablespoon minced scallions (white part only)

2 teaspoons minced garlic

¹/₂ pound pea shoots, tough stems removed, wilted leaves discarded, and cut into 2-inch lengths

¹/₄ cup Chinese rice wine or sake

5¹/₂ cups Chinese Chicken Broth (page 53)

1¹/₂ teaspoons salt, or to taste

1. Divide the noodles equally among six soup bowls.

2. In a medium bowl, combine the shrimp with the rice wine and ginger, tossing lightly to coat.

3. Heat a heavy pot over medium-high heat. Add the oil and heat until hot, about 30 seconds. Add the scallions and garlic and stir-fry for 15 seconds, or until fragrant. Add the pea shoots and rice wine, turn up the heat to high, and stir-fry for 30 seconds. Add the broth and salt and bring to a boil. Add the shrimp and simmer for about 1¹/₂ minutes, until they turn pink, skimming the broth to remove any foam or impurities. Taste for seasoning, ladle the soup over the noodles, and serve.

6 SERVINGS

Thai Clam Pot

No seafood captures the fresh, briny flavor of the ocean better than clams. I usually cook them simply, with a little garlic and rice wine. For a Thai variation, I add fresh basil and crushed red pepper. The resulting broth is spectacular and the clams are served over delicate somen noodles.

1 teaspoon safflower or corn oil

Spicy Seasonings Mix together
1 teaspoon crushed red pepper
8 cloves garlic, smashed and thinly sliced
8 scallions, trimmed, cut into 1 1/2-inch lengths, and smashed lightly with the flat side of a knife

1 1/2 cups water
3/4 cup Chinese rice wine or sake
3 pounds littleneck clams, preferably small, scrubbed, soaked in cold water to cover for 1 hour, and drained
1/4 pound somen or other very thin noodles, such as angel hair, cooked until just tender, rinsed under warm water, and drained
1 cup Thai holy basil or sweet basil leaves, finely shredded
2 tablespoons fish sauce, or to taste

1. Heat a large heavy pot over high heat. Add the oil and heat until hot, about 30 seconds. Add spicy seasonings and stir-fry for about 10 seconds, or until fragrant. Add the water and rice wine, cover, and bring to a boil. Add the clams, cover, and bring to a boil. Reduce the heat to medium and cook, shaking the pot from time to time so the clams cook evenly for 8 minutes, or just until the clams open.
2. Meanwhile, divide the noodles equally among six soup bowls.
3. Add the basil to the clams, stir gently, cover, and cook for 30 seconds. Add the fish sauce. Ladle the clams and broth into the bowls and serve immediately.

6 SERVINGS

60

Seafood Hot Pot

THINK OF THIS AS A CHINESE BOUILLABAISSE—flowing over with chunks of fish, nuggets of scallops, and plump shrimp. Ladle the seafood and fragrant broth over the noodles and season with spicy hot-and-sour Mongolian sauce for a memorable feast.

¹/₂ pound medium shrimp, peeled, scored down the back, deveined, and rinsed

¹/₂ pound scallops, rinsed and drained

I pound firm-fleshed white fish fillets, such as haddock, red snapper, or orange roughy, cut into I-inch chunks

Seafood Marinade **Whisk together**

¹/₃ cup Chinese rice wine or sake

I ¹/₂ tablespoons minced fresh ginger

I ¹/₂ teaspoons toasted sesame oil

¹/₂ pound flat Chinese wheat-flour noodles, udon, or other flat noodles, such as fettuccine, cooked until just tender, rinsed under warm water, and drained

I teaspoon safflower or corn oil

4 cloves garlic, peeled and lightly smashed with the flat side of a knife

I small Napa cabbage, cut into 2-inch squares, stem and tender leafy sections separated

¹/₃ cup Chinese rice wine or sake

5 cups Chinese Chicken Broth (page 53)

I ¹/₂ teaspoons salt

2 tablespoons minced scallion greens

Mongolian Sauce (page 121)

1. Place the seafood in three separate bowls, divide the seafood marinade among the bowls, and toss lightly to coat. Divide the noodles among six soup bowls.

2. Heat a Dutch oven or a casserole over high heat. Add the oil and heat until almost smoking hot, about 30 seconds. Add the garlic and cabbage stems and stir-fry until the cabbage is slightly limp, about 1 minute. Add the rice wine, toss lightly, cover, and cook for 1 ¹/₂ minutes. Add the remaining cabbage and the broth, partially cover, and bring to a boil. Uncover, reduce the heat, and simmer for 30 minutes.

3. Add the salt and stir well. Arrange the seafood on top of the cabbage, in three separate piles. Cover and cook for 5 to 7 minutes, just until the shrimp are pink and the scallops and fish are opaque throughout. Sprinkle the scallions on top. To serve, spoon the seafood mixture and broth over the noodles and pass the Mongolian sauce.

6 SERVINGS

Cinnamon Beef Noodles

THIS IS THE DISH I CRAVE WHEN I AM FEELING A COLD or the flu coming on—a big bowl of noodles topped with spinach and tender pieces of beef infused with garlic, ginger, anise, and cinnamon. The flavor gets better and better every time you reheat it.

1 teaspoon safflower or corn oil

Chile-Cinnamon Seasonings

6 scallions, trimmed, cut into 1½-inch sections, and smashed lightly with the flat side of a knife

6 cloves garlic, peeled, smashed lightly with the flat side of a cleaver, and thinly sliced

4 slices fresh ginger (about the size of a quarter), smashed lightly with the flat side of a knife

1½ teaspoons hot chile paste

2 cinnamon sticks

1 teaspoon aniseed

8½ cups water

½ cup soy sauce

2 pounds chuck or beef stew meat, trimmed of fat and gristle, and cut into 1½-inch cubes

10-ounces spinach, trimmed, rinsed, and drained

½ pound flat Chinese wheat-flour noodles, udon, or other flat noodles, such as fettuccine, cooked until just tender, rinsed under warm water, and drained

3 tablespoons minced scallions

1. Heat a large pot or casserole over medium-high heat. Add the oil and heat until hot, about 30 seconds. Add the chile-cinnamon seasonings and stir-fry until fragrant, about 15 seconds. Add the water and soy sauce and bring to a boil. Add the beef and bring back to a boil. Reduce the heat to low, cover, and simmer for 1½ hours, or until the beef is very tender. Skim the surface to remove any impurities or fat. Remove the ginger slices and cinnamon sticks and discard. Add the spinach and bring to a boil.
2. Divide the noodles among six soup bowls. Ladle the meat, spinach, and broth over the noodles and sprinkle with the scallions. Serve.

6 SERVINGS

Scallion Chicken with Soba Soup

ONE TASTE OF THIS SOUP AND I AM TRANSPORTED back to the Kanda Yabusoba restaurant in Tokyo, where the noodles are still made by hand as they have been since 1860. The broth is soothing and the noodles are light and clean. Fresh handmade soba is superior to the dried variety, but either type will work here.

1 pound boneless, skinless chicken breasts, cut into
$^1/_6$-inch-thick slices

Soy-Ginger Marinade **Mix together**

3$^1/_2$ tablespoons soy sauce

1$^1/_2$ tablespoons Chinese rice wine or sake

1 tablespoon minced fresh ginger

$^1/_2$ pound soba, cooked until just tender, rinsed under warm water, and drained

6 cups Japanese Broth (page 54)

$^1/_4$ cup mirin (sweetened rice wine)

3 tablespoons soy sauce

1 cup thinly sliced scallions (cut on the diagonal into $^1/_4$-inch lengths)

3 tablespoons coarsely chopped toasted walnuts

1. In a bowl, combine the chicken with the soy-ginger marinade, tossing lightly to coat. Divide the noodles among six soup bowls.

2. In a casserole or a Dutch oven, combine the broth, mirin, and soy sauce and bring to a gentle boil over medium-high heat. Add the chicken and marinade and cook for 4 to 5 minutes, or until cooked through and tender. Skim any impurities from the surface, add the scallions, and cook for 1 minute.

3. Spoon the chicken, scallions, and hot broth over the noodles. Sprinkle with the chopped walnuts and serve.

6 SERVINGS

Thai Beef with Mint Soup

CINNAMON STICK, STAR ANISE, AND GINGER are combined with beef bones to create an irresistible stock for plump rice noodles. Mint leaves are tossed in at the last minute, creating a hearty soup that is fresh and satisfying in both fair and foul weather.

3 pounds beef shinbones or oxtails, preferably with meat and marrow

Ginger-Anise Seasonings
6 slices fresh ginger (about the size of a quarter), peeled and smashed lightly with the flat side of a knife
6 scallions, trimmed and smashed lightly with the flat side of a knife
1 cinnamon stick
2 stars anise

12 cups water

Broth Seasonings Mix together
4¹/₂ tablespoons fish sauce
3 tablespoons soy sauce
1 teaspoon sugar
¹/₄ teaspoon freshly ground black pepper

1 teaspoon safflower or corn oil
¹/₄ cup thinly sliced garlic
5¹/₂ ounces flat rice noodles, softened in hot water, cooked until just tender, rinsed under warm water, and drained
¹/₂ pound boneless beef sirloin, trimmed of fat and gristle and cut into paper-thin slices about 1-inch square
1¹/₂ cups bean sprouts, rinsed and drained
1 cup fresh mint leaves, finely shredded

1. Combine the beef bones, ginger-anise seasonings, and water in a large pot and bring to a boil. Turn down the heat to low and simmer, uncovered, for 1¹/₂ hours, skimming any impurities and fat from the surface.

2. Strain the broth into another large pot. Remove any meat from the bones and cut into thin slices; discard the bones and seasonings. Add the broth seasonings and the cooked meat to the broth and keep warm over low heat.

3. Heat a small frying pan over medium-high heat. Add the oil and heat until hot, about 30 seconds. Add the garlic and stir-fry until lightly golden. Remove from the heat.

4. Divide the noodles among six soup bowls.

5. Add the uncooked beef to the hot broth and stir to separate the slices. Add the bean sprouts and mint leaves and bring almost to a boil. Skim the surface to remove any impurities, and ladle the beef and broth over the noodles. Sprinkle the fried garlic on top and serve.

6 SERVINGS

Mushroom-Beef Udon Soup

THICK, SMOOTH UDON NOODLES OFTEN GARNISH SUKIYAKI, a hearty soup pot of beef, chicken, shrimp, and vegetables. This simplified version mingles beef, spinach, and dried and fresh shiitake mushrooms. It's just the thing for a cozy winter meal.

1. In a bowl, combine the beef with the soy sauce and mirin, tossing to coat.

2. In a large pot or a casserole, heat the oil over medium-high heat until hot, about 30 seconds. Add the black mushrooms and stir-fry until fragrant, about 10 seconds. Add the fresh mushrooms and the scallions and stir-fry for 1½ minutes. Add the reserved mushroom soaking liquid and the broth and bring to a boil. Reduce the heat to low and simmer for 5 to 7 minutes. Add the beef slices, stir to separate them, and cook until the beef loses its pink color, about 2 minutes. Skim the surface to remove any impurities.

3. Add the soy sauce and spinach and cook just until the spinach wilts.

4. Divide the noodles among six soup bowls, spoon the soup on top, and serve.

6 SERVINGS

1 pound boneless beef sirloin or beef tenderloin, trimmed of fat and gristle and cut into ¹/₆-inch-thick slices

3 tablespoons soy sauce

2¹/₂ tablespoons mirin (sweetened rice wine) or 2¹/₂ tablespoons Chinese rice wine or sake plus 1¹/₂ teaspoons sugar

1 teaspoon toasted sesame oil

6 dried Chinese black mushrooms, softened in 1 cup hot water, drained (reserve the soaking liquid), stems removed, and caps thinly sliced

¹/₂ pound shiitake mushrooms, rinsed, drained, stems removed, and caps thinly sliced

1¹/₂ cups ¹/₄-inch lengths scallions

4 cups Japanese Broth (page 54)

2 tablespoons soy sauce

¹/₂ pound spinach, trimmed, rinsed, and drained

¹/₂ pound thick round noodles, udon, wheat-flour noodles, or spaghettini, cooked until just tender, rinsed under warm water, and drained.

69

Hanoi Beef Noodles (Pho)

THIS IS THE VIETNAMESE EQUIVALENT OF CHICKEN SOUP and one of the most celebrated in Vietnam. The fragrant stock is infused with cinnamon, anise, and ginger—the ultimate soothing spices. Eat it as the Vietnamese do—at any time of day, for breakfast, lunch, or dinner.

Beef Stock

3³/₄ pounds of beef shinbones or oxtails, preferably with meat and marrow

16 cups water

4 shallots, thinly sliced

6 slices fresh ginger (about the size of a quarter), peeled and smashed lightly with the flat side of a knife

4 stars anise

2 cinnamon sticks

¹/₄ cup fish sauce

¹/₄ teaspoon freshly ground black pepper

6 ounces thin flat rice stick noodles (pho), softened in hot water, cooked until just tender, rinsed under warm water, and drained

1 lime, cut into 6 wedges

1 hot red chile pepper, thinly sliced into rings

¹/₂ pound boneless beef sirloin, trimmed of fat and gristle and cut into paper-thin slices about 1¹/₂ inches square

2 cups bean sprouts, rinsed and drained

Garnishes

¹/₄ cup minced scallion greens

¹/₄ cup minced fresh cilantro

1 cup Thai holy basil or sweet basil leaves, shredded

1. In a large pot, combine the beef stock ingredients and bring to a boil. Turn down the heat to low and simmer, uncovered, for 1¹/₂ hours, skimming any impurities and fat from the surface.

2. Strain the broth into another large pot. Remove any meat from the bones and cut into thin slices; discard the bones and the stock seasonings. Skim any fat from the surface of the stock. Add the fish sauce and black pepper and keep warm over low heat.

3. Divide the noodles among six soup bowls. Put the lime wedges on a small plate and put the chile pepper in a small bowl.

4. Add the cooked sliced beef, the sirloin, and bean sprouts to the hot soup, bring to a boil, and cook until the sirloin loses its pink color, 1¹/₂ to 2 minutes. Skim the surface to remove any impurities.

5. Ladle the beef, bean sprouts, and broth over the noodles. Sprinkle the scallions, cilantro, and basil on top. Serve with the lime slices and chile pepper for seasoning.

6 SERVINGS

most memorable recipes for these salads have been concocted from whatever is in my refrigerator on a given day or whatever catches my eye at the
market. I especially love to create my own interpretations of traditional
dishes. Since I'm a huge fan of wilted salads, I toss spinach, fresh crabmeat,
and diced bell peppers in a warm soy dressing. I also like to grill seafood or
meat and serve it with a mixture of stir-fried vegetables over noodles to
create a mouthwatering entrée. The dressings are light and spicy.

In these salads, the noodles—which can be almost any type (I often
take advantage of the fresh egg and vegetable pastas sold in supermarkets)—
provide bulk and textural contrast to the other ingredients. Cut-up vegetables, such as bell peppers, cucumbers, snow peas, carrots, and bean
sprouts, offer colorful mosaic patterns, while poached, grilled, or stir-fried
meats and seafood add substance. As for the dressings, fresh lemon or lime
juice and rice wine vinegar are the key elements in many, with toasted
sesame oil, soy sauce, or fish sauce rounding out the flavors. Pungent seasonings—garlic, ginger, chile peppers, scallions, lemongrass, cilantro, basil,
and mint—add vibrancy and freshness.

Noodle salads are not only visually spectacular, they are also the
ideal entrée, since they easily become *the* whole meal. I've included some
of my favorite recipes here to give you a taste of the endless possibilities.

74

Wilted Spinach and Crab Salad

I LOVE WARM SALADS WITH GREENS that are lightly cooked to eliminate the raw, slightly bitter edge. Here, leafy spinach, nuggets of fresh crabmeat, and diced bell peppers are bathed in a tart dressing. One mouthful delivers an incomparable textural experience—crisp, smooth, and tangy. If fresh crabmeat is unavailable, make the salad with cooked medium shrimp.

1. Heat a wok or a heavy skillet over high heat. Add the oil and heat until hot, about 30 seconds. Add the scallion-ginger seasonings and toss lightly until fragrant, about 15 seconds. Add the red peppers and rice wine and toss lightly until crisp-tender, about 1 minute.

2. Add the rice vinegar dressing and bring to a boil. Add the spinach and crabmeat and toss lightly until the spinach is lightly wilted, about 30 seconds. Remove to a serving bowl. Sprinkle with the crisp fried noodles and serve immediately.

6 SERVINGS

1 tablespoon safflower or corn oil

Scallion-Ginger Seasonings
3 tablespoons minced scallion greens
1 1/2 tablespoons minced fresh ginger
1 1/2 tablespoons minced garlic

2 red bell peppers, cored, seeded, and cut into 1/4-inch dice
2 tablespoons Chinese rice wine or sake

Rice Vinegar Dressing Mix together
6 tablespoons soy sauce
1 1/2 tablespoons sugar
3 1/2 tablespoons Japanese rice vinegar

About 20 ounces spinach, trimmed, rinsed, drained, and torn into large pieces
1 pound fresh lump crabmeat, picked through to remove shells and cartilage
1 ounce cellophane noodles (bean threads), deep-fried as on page 11 and crumbled

Red-Hot Sichuan Noodles

MY HUSBAND CRAVES THE HOT CHILE OIL that makes these noodles addictive. It's so easy to put together: You simply steep garlic, ginger, and dried chile peppers in heated oil. Mix and match different vegetables and cooked seafood and meats to create infinite variations of this salad.

1¹/₂ pounds medium shrimp, peeled, scored down the back, deveined, rinsed, and patted dry

Scallion-Ginger Marinade **Mix together**
2¹/₂ tablespoons **Chinese rice wine or sake**
2 tablespoons minced **scallions (white part only)**
1¹/₂ tablespoons minced fresh **ginger**

³/₄ pound flat **Chinese egg noodles or other flat noodles, such as fettuccine, cooked until just tender, rinsed under cold water, and drained**
2 English (seedless) **cucumbers, peeled, halved lengthwise, seeded, cut into ¹/₂-inch-long shreds or shredded in the food processor, and squeezed dry**
5 carrots, peeled and cut into 1¹/₂-inch-long shreds or shredded in the food processor
1¹/₂ cups bean sprouts, rinsed and drained
1¹/₂ cups ¹/₂-inch lengths scallion greens
Red-Hot Chile Oil Dressing (page 118)

1. In a bowl, combine the shrimp with the scallion-ginger marinade and toss to coat.
2. Bring a saucepan of water to a boil. Add the shrimp and cook for about 3 minutes, until they turn pink; drain.
3. Arrange the noodles on a platter. Arrange the shredded vegetables randomly or in concentric circles on top of the noodles, leaving a space in the center. Scatter the bean sprouts and scallions over the vegetables and arrange the shrimp in the center. Serve at room temperature or cold, with the red-hot chile oil dressing.

6 SERVINGS

76

Grilled Seafood Salad

THE DOG DAYS OF SUMMER INSPIRE ME TO CREATE no-fuss meal-in-one salads like this one. Scallops and shrimp, seasoned with rice wine, ginger, soy sauce, and sesame oil, are quickly seared and served over crisp-cooked snow peas and sweet peppers, nestled on a bed of noodles. The whole platter is drizzled with a spunky cilantro–sesame oil vinaigrette.

I pound medium shrimp, peeled, scored down the back, deveined, rinsed, and patted dry

I pound sea scallops, rinsed, drained, and sliced in half horizontally

Seafood Marinade Mix together
3¹/₂ tablespoons soy sauce
1¹/₂ teaspoons toasted sesame oil
¹/₂ cup Chinese rice wine or sake
3 tablespoons minced fresh ginger

³/₄ pound flat egg or spinach noodles, such as linguine or fettuccine, cooked until just tender, rinsed under cold water, drained, and tossed with
I teaspoon toasted sesame oil

I tablespoon safflower or corn oil

2 red bell peppers, cored, seeded, and cut into thin strips

3 tablespoons minced scallion greens

1¹/₂ tablespoons minced garlic

³/₄ pound snow peas, ends snapped and strings removed

1¹/₂ tablespoons Chinese rice wine or sake

Cilantro Vinaigrette (page 121)

Twenty 10-inch bamboo skewers (soaked in water for I hour) or metal skewers

1. In a medium bowl, toss the shrimp with half the seafood marinade. In another bowl, toss the scallops with the remaining marinade. Let sit for 20 minutes, then thread the shrimp and scallops separately onto the skewers.

2. Prepare a medium-hot fire for grilling or heat the broiler.

3. Arrange the noodles in a serving bowl.

4. Heat a wok or a skillet over high heat. Add the oil and heat until hot, about 30 seconds. Add the red peppers, scallions, and garlic and toss lightly for 1¹/₂ minutes. Add the snow peas and rice wine and cook until crisp-tender, about 2 minutes. Arrange the vegetables over the noodles.

5. Grill or broil the seafood for 3 to 4 minutes on each side, until the shrimp are pink and the scallops are cooked through. Remove from the skewers and arrange on the vegetables and noodles. Drizzle the cilantro vinaigrette over all.

6 SERVINGS

Rainbow Peanut Noodles

I'M INVITED TO NEIGHBORHOOD PARTIES not for my witty conversation but for my peanut noodles. In fact, I started a craze when I served this noodle salad at a street gathering. Everyone demanded the recipe and soon it appeared in different forms at every neighborhood get-together. The spicy peanut dressing is superb on almost any salad. During the summer, I keep extra on hand and always have a package of noodles and some vegetables in my refrigerator for a cool, ready-in-minutes meal.

1/2 pound thin noodles, such as linguine, cooked until just tender, rinsed under cold water, drained, and tossed with 1 teaspoon toasted sesame oil

5 carrots, peeled and grated

2 English (seedless) cucumbers, peeled, halved lengthwise, seeded, shredded, and squeezed dry

2 cups bean sprouts, rinsed and drained

1 red bell pepper, cored, seeded, and cut into thin strings (about 1 cup)

2 cups sliced cooked chicken (cut into thin strips)

1 1/2 tablespoons minced scallion greens

Chinese Peanut Dressing (page 122)

1. Arrange the noodles in a large serving bowl.
2. Arrange the vegetables in concentric circles over the noodles and then pile the chicken in the center. Sprinkle the scallions on top.
3. Serve at room temperature or chilled, with the Chinese peanut dressing.

6 SERVINGS

Spicy Pesto Soba

THE JAPANESE CONSIDER SOBA NOODLES a tonic for the body. Toss them with a fresh herb pesto of garlic, fresh basil, and mint and they become a superb restorative.

1/2 pound snow peas, ends snapped, strings removed, sliced lengthwise in half

3/4 pound soba noodles, cooked until just tender, rinsed under cold water, and drained

Spicy Pesto Blend to a paste in a food processor or a blender

1 to 2 hot red chile peppers or 1 teaspoon crushed red pepper

6 cloves garlic

1 cup fresh basil leaves

1/2 cup fresh mint leaves

1 tablespoon toasted sesame oil

1 pound boneless, skinless chicken breasts, cooked and cut into thin strips

3/4 cup minced scallion greens

Rice Wine Dressing Whisk together

1/2 cup plus 1 tablespoon soy sauce

6 tablespoons Japanese rice vinegar

3 tablespoons sugar

2 tablespoons mirin (sweetened rice wine) or 2 tablespoons Chinese rice wine or sake plus 1 tablespoon sugar

1. Bring a large pot of water to a boil. Add the snow peas and blanch for 10 seconds. Drain, refresh in cold water, and drain again. Blot dry with paper towels.

2. In a bowl, toss together the noodles and the spicy pesto. Arrange the noodles on a platter and arrange the snow peas, chicken, and scallions in concentric circles on top, with the chicken and scallions in the center. Serve the dressing on the side or sprinkle the dressing on top and toss lightly.

6 SERVINGS

Warm Garlic Beef and Cellophane Noodle Salad

GRILLED MARINATED FLANK STEAK WAS ONE OF MY childhood summer favorites. Then, the marinade was bottled Italian dressing. Now *I* make it—soy sauce mixed with a little sugar and *lots* of smashed garlic, scallions, and red pepper—and the sliced beef and vegetable on a bed of noodles are delicious.

1 1/2 pounds flank steak or London broil, trimmed of fat or gristle

Sesame Garlic Marinade

1/2 cup soy sauce

1/3 cup Chinese rice wine or sake

2 tablespoons sugar

10 cloves garlic, peeled and smashed with the flat side of a knife

10 scallions, trimmed and smashed with the flat side of a knife

1 teaspoon crushed red pepper

1 teaspoon toasted sesame oil

One 3 1/2-ounce package cellophane noodles (bean threads), softened in hot water, cooked until just tender, rinsed under cold water, drained, and cut into 3-inch lengths

1 pound green beans, trimmed, cut on the diagonal into 2-inch lengths, blanched in boiling water until crisp-tender, refreshed in cold water, and drained

Chinese Garlic Dressing (page 118)

1 teaspoon safflower or corn oil if pan-searing the beef

3 tablespoons minced scallion greens

1. Put the steak in a shallow dish. In a saucepan, mix the marinade ingredients, bring to boil, reduce heat to low, and simmer 5 minutes. Cool slightly; pour over the meat, tossing to coat. Marinate 1 hour at room temperature, or cover to refrigerate overnight.

2. Arrange the noodles on a platter. Put the green beans on top, leaving an indentation in the center. Spoon the garlic dressing over all.

3. Prepare a hot fire in a grill or heat a heavy skillet over high heat. Add the oil to the hot skillet and swirl to coat the surface. Grill the steak 5 to 7 minutes each side for medium-rare, or panfry 4 to 5 minutes each side. Let the meat rest on a cutting board 5 minutes. Cut across the grain into very thin slices.

4. Strain the marinade. Add half to the skillet and boil until it is reduced by half. Add the beef slices and toss lightly to coat. Arrange the slices in the center of the platter and over the beans and sprinkle with scallion greens.

6 SERVINGS

peanuts. Singapore Fried Rice Noodles are studded with luscious bits of shrimp, bell peppers, leeks, and bean sprouts, all seasoned with a hint of curry. In Curried Coconut Shrimp on Rice Noodles, aromatic seasonings such as lemongrass, ginger, cumin, coriander, and fresh basil are mixed with coconut milk and stir-fried with rice vermicelli, shrimp, and vegetables. The noodles are light but satisfying and the vibrant flavors are eminently appealing. All of these noodle dishes are perfect for busy cooks who have limited time but want to serve healthy, unique, and delicious meals.

92

Singapore Fried Rice Noodles

ON A RECENT TRIP TO SINGAPORE, I found myself returning again and again to the same hawker's stall for these noodles. A touch of curry powder gently seasons the noodles, which are interlaced with crisp-tender leeks, bell peppers, bean sprouts, and shrimp. Barbecued pork and other vegetables are often added to the mix but you can customize yours according to taste.

1. In a bowl, combine the shrimp with the ginger marinade, tossing to coat.

2. Heat a wok or a heavy skillet over high heat. Add 2 tablespoons of the oil and heat until hot, about 30 seconds. Add the shrimp and stir-fry until they turn pink, about 1 1/2 minutes. Remove with a handled strainer or a slotted spoon and drain in a colander. Wipe out the wok.

3. Reheat the wok, add the remaining 1 1/2 tablespoons oil and heat until very hot, about 20 seconds. Add the curry powder and stir-fry until fragrant. Add the leeks and ginger and stir-fry for about 1 1/2 minutes, until slightly limp. Add the bean sprouts and cook for 20 seconds, add the shrimp, rice noodles, and the Singapore sauce and toss gently until the noodles have absorbed the sauce and are tender. Transfer to a platter and serve.

6 SERVINGS

I pound medium shrimp, peeled, scored down the back, deveined, and rinsed

Ginger Marinade **Mix together**
2 tablespoons Chinese rice wine or sake
2 teaspoons minced fresh ginger
1/2 teaspoon toasted sesame oil

3 1/2 tablespoons safflower or corn oil
1 1/2 tablespoons curry powder, preferably Madras
3 1/2 cups finely shredded leeks
1 1/2 tablespoons minced fresh ginger
3 cups bean sprouts, rinsed and drained
1/4 pound thin rice stick noodles (vermicelli), softened in hot water and drained

Singapore Sauce **Mix together**
1/4 cup Chinese Chicken Broth (page 53) or water
2 tablespoons soy sauce
1/2 teaspoon sugar
I teaspoon salt
1/2 teaspoon freshly ground black pepper

Pad Thai

I AM ADDICTED TO GOOD PAD THAI. This classic Thai noodle stir-fry will hook you, too, with its delicate, slim noodles twisted around plump shrimp and crunchy bean sprouts, dressed in a sweet-and-sour sauce, and topped with crunchy peanuts and fresh cilantro. For a lighter version, use thin round rice stick noodles.

¹/₄ cup safflower or corn oil

I pound medium shrimp, peeled, scored down the back, deveined, and rinsed

3 large eggs, lightly beaten

2 tablespoons minced garlic

Sweet-and-Sour Sauce Mix together

¹/₃ cup fish sauce

¹/₄ cup ketchup

I¹/₂ tablespoons sugar

3 tablespoons water

6 ounces flat rice stick noodles (pho), softened in hot water and drained

2 cups bean sprouts, rinsed and drained

Garnishes

3 tablespoons minced scallion greens

¹/₄ cup finely chopped dry-roasted peanuts

¹/₂ teaspoon crushed red pepper

2¹/₂ tablespoons coarsely chopped fresh cilantro

2 limes, cut into 6 wedges each

1. Heat a wok or a heavy skillet over high heat. Add 1 tablespoon of the oil and heat until very hot, about 30 seconds. Add the shrimp and stir-fry until they turn pink, about 1¹/₂ minutes. Remove with a handled strainer or a slotted spoon and drain in a colander. Wipe out the wok.

2. Reheat the wok over medium-high heat. Add the remaining 3 tablespoons oil and heat until hot, about 30 seconds. Add the eggs and cook, stirring to scramble them, until just set. Add the garlic and stir-fry until fragrant, about 10 seconds. Add the sweet-and-sour sauce and the rice noodles and toss for 3 to 4 minutes, until the noodles have absorbed the sauce and are tender. Add the shrimp and bean sprouts and toss to mix. Transfer onto a serving platter and sprinkle with the scallion greens, peanuts, red pepper, and cilantro. Arrange the lime wedges around the noodles and serve.

6 SERVINGS

Curried Coconut Shrimp on Rice Noodles

OF ALL OF THE CURRY MIXTURES I MAKE, this one is the most vibrant. The intensity comes from the lemongrass. When pungent seasonings like coriander, cumin, ginger, chile peppers, and lemongrass are ground in a food processor or a spice blender, their flavors come to life. Use this curry mixture as well in marinades for any grilled seafood or chicken.

6 ounces thin rice stick noodles (vermicelli), softened in hot water, cooked until just tender, rinsed under cold water, and drained

1 1/2 tablespoons safflower or corn oil

Fragrant Seasonings Process to a coarse powder in a food processor or a blender

3 dried red chile peppers or 1 1/2 teaspoons crushed red pepper

2 stalks lemongrass, trimmed, wilted or tough outer leaves discarded, and cut into 2-inch lengths

One 1 1/2-inch piece fresh ginger, peeled and cut in half

1 1/2 teaspoons ground cumin

1 1/2 teaspoons ground coriander

1 teaspoon salt

1/2 teaspoon freshly ground black pepper

2 red onions, cut into thin strips

Coconut Sauce Mix together

1 1/2 cups coconut milk

3 tablespoons fish sauce

1 tablespoon sugar

1 1/2 pounds medium shrimp, peeled, scored down the back, deveined, and rinsed

1 1/2 cups frozen peas, thawed

1 cup fresh basil leaves, cut into thin strips

1. Arrange the noodles on a platter or in a serving bowl.

2. Heat a wok or a heavy skillet over medium-high heat. Add the oil and heat until hot, about 30 seconds. Add the fragrant seasonings and the onions, turn the heat down to medium-low, and stir-fry for 3 to 4 minutes, until the onions are tender. Add the coconut sauce and cook for 3 minutes more. Add the shrimp, turn up the heat to medium-high, and cook for 2 to 3 minutes, until the shrimp turn pink. Add the peas and basil, toss lightly, and spoon over the rice stick noodles. Serve.

6 SERVINGS

96

Crisp-Cooked Vegetarian Noodles

Even meat lovers will find this spicy noodle platter intoxicatingly good. To make it a trifle more substantial, marinate sliced tofu in a little soy sauce seasoned with minced ginger, garlic, sugar, and sesame oil, bake it for thirty-five minutes, and toss with the vegetables.

3/4 pound thin **Chinese egg noodles or angel hair,** cooked until just tender, rinsed under cold water, drained, and tossed with 1 teaspoon toasted sesame oil

1 tablespoon plus 2 teaspoons **safflower or corn oil**

Black Mushroom Seasonings Mix together

1 1/2 tablespoons **minced garlic**

1 tablespoon **minced fresh ginger**

12 dried **Chinese black mushrooms,** softened in 2 cups hot water, drained (reserve the soaking liquid), stems removed, and caps thinly sliced

6 **leeks,** trimmed, thoroughly cleaned, and cut into thin 1 1/2-inch-long strips

6 **carrots,** peeled and grated or shredded

1/4 cup **Chinese rice wine or sake**

Mushroom Sauce Mix together

Reserved black mushroom soaking liquid plus enough water to make 3 1/2 cups

4 1/2 tablespoons **soy sauce**

1 1/2 teaspoons **toasted sesame oil**

2 1/2 tablespoons **cornstarch**

1. Preheat the broiler. Spread the noodles on a cookie sheet that has been lightly oiled and broil for about 10 minutes on each side, or until golden brown. Keep warm in a preheated 200°F oven.

2. Heat a wok or a heavy skillet over high heat. Add the oil and heat until hot, about 20 seconds. Add the black mushroom seasonings and stir-fry until fragrant. Add the leeks and carrots and stir-fry for about 1 minute. Add the rice wine and cook for another minute. Add the mushroom sauce and cook, stirring constantly to prevent lumps, until thickened. Remove from the heat.

3. Spoon the vegetable mixture on top of the noodles and serve.

6 SERVINGS

Hot-and-Sour Shrimp Lo Mein

WHEN I WAS GROWING UP, "ordering Chinese" invariably meant lo mein noodles. The Cantonese lo mein I loved as a child, however, bears little resemblance to this bright, fresh, and virtually greaseless version. Whenever I'm feeling nostalgic, I toss noodles in this spicy sauce laced with garlic, vinegar, and hot chiles.

1 1/2 pounds medium shrimp, peeled, scored down the back, deveined, and rinsed

Ginger Marinade Mix together
3 tablespoons Chinese rice wine or sake
1 1/2 tablespoons minced fresh ginger
1 teaspoon toasted sesame oil

3 1/2 tablespoons safflower or corn oil
1 medium red onion, thinly sliced
2 1/2 tablespoons minced garlic
1 teaspoon hot chile paste
1 1/2 cups sliced canned water chestnuts, blanched in boiling water for 10 seconds, refreshed in cold water, drained, and patted dry
1/2 pound snow peas, ends snapped and strings removed

Hot-and-Sour Sauce Mix together
1 1/2 cups Chinese Chicken Broth (page 53) or water
5 1/2 tablespoons soy sauce
2 tablespoons Chinese rice wine or sake
2 tablespoons sugar
2 tablespoons Chinese black vinegar or Worchestershire sauce
1 teaspoon toasted sesame oil
1 tablespoon cornstarch

1/2 pound flat noodles, such as fettuccine or linguine, cooked until just tender, rinsed under cold water, and drained

1. In a bowl, combine the shrimp with the ginger marinade, tossing lightly to coat.

2. Heat a wok or a heavy skillet over high heat. Add 2 tablespoons of the oil and heat until very hot but not smoking. Add the shrimp and toss lightly for about 1 1/2 minutes until they turn pink. Remove with a handled strainer or a slotted spoon and drain in a colander. Wipe out the wok.

3. Reheat the wok over medium-high heat. Add the remaining 1 1/2 tablespoons of oil and heat until hot, about 20 seconds. Add the onion, garlic, and chile paste and stir-fry until the onion is slightly softened, 1 1/2 to 2 minutes. Add the water chestnuts and snow peas, turn up the heat to high, and toss until heated through. Add the hot-and-sour sauce and cook, stirring constantly to prevent lumps, until thickened, 2 to 3 minutes. Add the shrimp and noodles and mix gently. Transfer to a platter and serve immediately.

6 SERVINGS

Thai Basil Chicken with Rice Noodles

THAI HOLY, OR GRAPRAO BASIL, with smallish purple leaves, is even more intense in flavor than the familiar sweet basil. When the herb is seared in a hot pan, the basil's heady perfume is released. This basil is sold in Asian markets; if you can't find it, use sweet basil.

1 1/2 pounds boneless, skinless chicken breasts, cut into 1/6-inch thick slices

Shallot Marinade Mix together
3 tablespoons fish sauce
1 1/2 tablespoons Chinese rice wine or sake
1 1/2 tablespoons minced shallots

2 1/2 tablespoons safflower or corn oil

Peppery Seasonings Mix together
1 1/2 tablespoons chopped seeded hot red chile
2 tablespoons chopped garlic
2 large red bell peppers, cored, seeded, and thinly sliced
1 medium red onion, thinly sliced

Spicy Thai Sauce Mix together
5 tablespoons fish sauce
3 tablespoons soy sauce
3 tablespoons water
1 1/2 tablespoons sugar
1/4 teaspoon freshly ground black pepper

6 ounces thin rice stick noodles (vermicelli), softened in hot water and drained
1 1/2 cups fresh Thai holy basil or sweet basil leaves, coarsely shredded

1. In a bowl, combine the chicken slices with the shallot marinade, tossing lightly to coat.

2. Heat a wok or a heavy skillet over high heat. Add the oil and heat until very hot, about 30 seconds. Add the peppery seasonings and stir-fry for about 1 minute. Push the seasonings to one side, add the chicken, and stir-fry until the meat loses its pink color. Mix everything well and cook until the peppers are tender. Add the spicy Thai sauce and bring just to a boil, stirring constantly. Add the noodles and stir gently until they have absorbed the sauce and are tender. Add the basil and mix well. Transfer to a platter and serve.

6 SERVINGS

Seared Black Bean Chicken on Crisp Noodles

THIS IS A DISH I DREAM ABOUT—tender slices of chicken with red onions, peppers, and snow peas, all bathed in a garlicky black bean sauce and served over crisp noodles. I like to broil the noodles so that they are crisp on the outside and tender on the inside, and I often grill the chicken rather than panfry it.

Toasted Sesame Marinade Mix together

2 tablespoons minced garlic

3 tablespoons soy sauce

1 1/2 teaspoons toasted sesame oil

2 whole boneless, skinless chicken breasts (about 1 1/4 pounds), split

3/4 pound thin noodles, cooked, rinsed, drained, and tossed with 2 teaspoons toasted sesame oil

3 tablespoons safflower or corn oil

Black Bean Seasonings Mix together

2 tablespoons fermented (or salted) black beans, rinsed, drained, and minced

2 tablespoons minced garlic

1 1/2 tablespoons minced fresh ginger

1/2 teaspoon crushed red pepper (optional)

2 red onions, thinly sliced

2 red bell peppers, cored, seeded, and thinly sliced

1/2 pound snow peas, strings removed

Cantonese Sauce Mix together

2 cups Chinese Chicken Broth (page 53)

5 tablespoons soy sauce

1/4 cup Chinese rice wine or sake

1 1/2 tablespoons sugar

2 1/2 teaspoons cornstarch

1. Combine the marinade and chicken in a medium bowl; toss to coat.

2. Preheat the broiler. Spread the noodles on a baking sheet and broil for about 10 minutes on each side, or until golden brown. Transfer to a heat-proof serving platter and keep warm in a preheated 200°F oven.

3. Heat a heavy skillet over medium-high heat. Add 1 tablespoon of the oil and heat until hot, about 30 seconds. Add the chicken and cook for 6 to 7 minutes on each side, or until cooked thoroughly. Let cool slightly, then cut on the diagonal into thin slices.

4. Reheat the skillet over medium-high heat. Add the remaining 2 tablespoons oil and heat until hot, about 30 seconds. Add the black bean seasonings and stir-fry for about 2 minutes, until the onions and peppers are just tender. Add the snow peas and the Cantonese sauce and bring to a boil, stirring constantly to prevent lumps. Add the chicken and toss lightly to coat. Spoon over the noodles and serve.

6 SERVINGS

Garlic Beef with Shiitake Mushrooms on Golden Noodles

FEW DISHES ARE AS SEDUCTIVELY SUMPTUOUS as thin slices of beef, shiitake mushrooms, and snow peas bathed in a velvety oyster sauce on a bed of tender noodles. I've updated this Cantonese classic with fresh shiitake mushrooms rather than dried. For convenience, I sometimes broil the noodles (see page 18). You can substitute cremini mushrooms.

1 1/2 pounds flank steak, London broil, or boneless sirloin steak, trimmed of fat and gristle

Beef Marinade Mix together
3 1/2 tablespoons soy sauce
2 tablespoons Chinese rice wine or sake
2 tablespoons minced garlic
1 tablespoon cornstarch

5 1/2 tablespoons safflower or corn oil
1/2 pound shiitake mushrooms, rinsed, drained, stems removed, and caps thinly sliced
2 tablespoons minced garlic
1 1/2 tablespoons minced fresh ginger

3/4 pound Chinese snow peas, ends trimmed and strings removed
2 tablespoons Chinese rice wine or sake

Oyster Sauce Mix together
1 1/2 cups Chinese Chicken Broth (page 53)
6 tablespoons oyster sauce
1 1/2 tablespoons Chinese rice wine or sake
1 teaspoon soy sauce
1 teaspoon toasted sesame oil
1 1/2 tablespoons cornstarch

3/4 pound thin noodles, panfried (page 18) and kept warm in a low oven

1. Cut the meat into 1/6-inch-thick slices. In a bowl, combine them with the marinade, tossing lightly to coat.

2. Heat a wok or a heavy skillet over high heat. Add 3 1/2 tablespoons of the oil and heat until almost smoking hot. Add the beef slices and stir-fry over high heat until they lose their pink color and separate. Remove with a handled strainer or a slotted spoon and drain in a colander. Wipe out the wok.

3. Reheat the wok, add the remaining 2 tablespoons oil, and heat until hot, about 20 seconds. Add the mushrooms, garlic, and ginger and stir-fry for 1 minute. Add the snow peas and rice wine and stir-fry for 1 1/2 minutes. Add the oyster sauce and cook, stirring constantly to prevent lumps, until thickened. Add the beef and toss gently in the sauce. Spoon over the noodles and serve.

6 SERVINGS

Thai-Style Spicy Beef Jantaboon

THIN FLAT THAI RICE NOODLES, or jantaboon, are heftier than thin rice vermicelli. When they are stir-fried in a hot pan, the seared edges become slightly crisp, a delicious contrast to slices of beef and crunchy bean sprouts. A simple dusting of fresh cilantro and chopped peanuts makes this dish truly exceptional.

Garlicky Marinade
2 tablespoons soy sauce
1 tablespoon minced garlic
1 teaspoon sugar

1 pound lean flank steak, London broil, or boneless sirloin steak, trimmed of fat and gristle and cut into 1/6-inch-thick slices

3 1/2 tablespoons safflower or corn oil

Red-Hot Seasonings Mix together
1 tablespoon minced garlic
2 hot red chile peppers, seeded and cut into thin rings
2 cups 1-inch lengths scallion greens

3 cups bean sprouts, rinsed and drained

Fragrant Tossing Sauce Mix together
1/4 cup soy sauce
1/4 cup Chinese rice wine or sake
3 tablespoons fish sauce
3 tablespoons sugar

6 ounces medium flat rice noodles (jantaboon), softened in hot water, cooked until just tender, rinsed under warm water, and drained
1/4 cup coarsely chopped fresh cilantro
3 tablespoons chopped dry-roasted peanuts

1. Combine the garlicky marinade ingredients in a large bowl. Add the meat and toss to coat.
2. Heat a wok or a heavy skillet over high heat. Add 2 tablespoons of the oil and heat until almost smoking hot. Add the beef and stir-fry until the slices lose their pink color and separate. Remove with a handled strainer or a slotted spoon and drain in a colander. Wipe out the wok.
3. Reheat the wok, add the remaining 1 1/2 tablespoons oil, and heat until hot, about 20 seconds. Add the red-hot seasonings and stir-fry until fragrant, about 10 seconds. Add the bean sprouts, and toss lightly for 30 seconds. Add the fragrant tossing sauce, the noodles, and meat and toss lightly until the noodles absorb the sauce and are tender. Transfer to a platter, sprinkle with the cilantro and peanuts, and serve.

6 SERVINGS

110

Hearty Pork Noodles

WHEN I FIRST VISITED JAPAN SOME TWENTY YEARS AGO, during the middle of a bitter-cold winter, I sustained myself with visits to the communal hot baths and endless bowls of noodle soups and stews. One of the most memorable is this dish of tender pork pieces with scallions braised in soy sauce.

2 teaspoons safflower or corn oil

2 pounds boneless pork loin or pork butt, trimmed of fat and gristle and cut into 1 1/2-inch cubes

12 scallions, trimmed, cut into 3- to 4-inch lengths, and mashed lightly with the flat side of a knife

8 slices fresh ginger (about the size of a quarter), mashed lightly with the flat side of a knife

Rich Braising Liquid **Mix together**

2 1/2 cups water

3/4 cup Chinese rice wine or sake

1/2 cup soy sauce

3 tablespoons sugar

1 pound bok choy, collard greens, or spinach, trimmed, rinsed, and dried

8 ounces ramen, thin Chinese egg noodles, or spaghettini, cooked until just tender, rinsed under warm water, and drained

1. In a casserole or Dutch oven, heat 1 teaspoon of the oil over high heat until hot, about 30 seconds. Add half the pork cubes and sear until brown on all sides. Transfer to a plate. Heat the remaining 1 teaspoon oil and sear the remaining meat. Remove to the plate.

2. Add the scallions and ginger to the hot pot and toss briefly. Add the rich braising liquid and bring to a boil. Add the pork, reduce the heat to low, and simmer, partially covered, for 1 hour, or until very tender.

3. Skim off any fat and impurities from the broth. Remove the pork and let cool slightly. Remove and discard the ginger. Cut the pieces of the pork in half, return to the pot, and keep warm over low heat.

4. Place the greens in a saucepan, add 1/4 cup water, cover, and cook until just tender, 2 to 3 minutes. Refresh in cold water and drain.

5. Divide the noodles among six soup bowls. Top with the cooked greens, spoon the meat and broth over, and serve.

6 SERVINGS

112

Spunky Stir-fried Ramen

WALK AROUND ANY CITY OR TOWN IN JAPAN and you will see some version of this dish. When I'm rushed, which is most of the time, I use the instant "ramen," discarding the flavor package, dipping the noodles in boiling water, and tossing them quickly in the sauce.

1. In a bowl, mix the meat with the marinade, toss lightly, and let marinate for 30 minutes.

2. Heat a wok or a skillet, add 3 tablespoons of oil, and heat until near smoking. Add the pork, stir-fry until the shreds separate and change color, remove, and drain. Wipe out the pan and reheat.

3. Add the remaining oil and heat over high heat until hot. Add the onions and crushed pepper, and stir-fry about 1 minute. Add the cabbage shreds. Toss lightly for 1 minute and add the carrots and rice wine. Cook for another minute and add the sauce. Heat until boiling. Add the cooked pork and the noodles, and toss lightly to blend. Transfer to a platter and serve immediately.

6 SERVINGS

I pound boneless center-cut pork loin, fat trimmed and cut into thin julienne strips

Marinade **Mix together**
2 tablespoons soy sauce
1 1/2 tablespoons minced gingerroot
I tablespoon minced garlic

4 1/2 tablespoons safflower or corn oil
2 cups sliced onions, cut into thin julienne shreds
I teaspoon crushed red pepper, or to taste
4 cups sliced Chinese Napa cabbage, stem section trimmed, slices laid flat and cut lengthwise in half, then into thin julienne shreds, leaf and stem sections separated
I cup grated carrots
1 1/2 tablespoons rice wine or sake

Sauce **Mix together**
1/4 cup soy sauce
3 tablespoons rice wine or sake
1 1/2 tablespoons sugar
1 1/2 tablespoons Worcestershire sauce
1/2 teaspoon toasted sesame seeds

3/4 pound fine dried Japanese *ramen*, Chinese egg noodles, or angel hair pasta, cooked until just tender, rinsed, and drained

113

Dipping Sauces and Dressings

PERHAPS NO OTHER ACCOMPANIMENTS complement and accessorize dishes better than Asian dipping sauces and dressings. A peanut sauce or spicy sesame dressing elevates a simple salad of cold chicken with vegetables and noodles from ordinary to exceptional. Crisp lettuce, tender rice vermicelli, and grilled chicken or meat take on a whole new dimension when paired with a creamy coconut-peanut satay sauce. Similarly, a hot-and-sour Mongolian sauce infused with the flavorings of ginger, scallions, garlic, and chile paste turns a seafood hot pot of shrimp, scallops, and fish into a memorable meal.

Asian sauces and dressings rely on ingredients such as rice vinegar, lime or lemon juice, fish sauce, toasted sesame oil, garlic, fresh ginger, mint, and cilantro and other herbs to stimulate the palate and get the juices flowing. None of the recipes here is set in stone, and I encourage you to improvise with whatever ingredients are available. If Chinese black vinegar is nowhere to be found, use Worcestershire sauce. If fish sauce is unavailable, use soy sauce instead.

Most of the sauces and dressings in this chapter can be prepared in advance and will keep for some time. Don't be afraid to mix and match these sauces or dressings with dishes that aren't Asian—they go with a lot of things. I often pair Chinese, Thai, and Vietnamese sauces with different kinds of food to create completely new dishes.

Red-Hot Chile Oil Dressing

I NEVER USE STORE-BOUGHT CHILE OIL; it doesn't carry anywhere near the flavor of homemade. What's more, some brands add food coloring to give the oil a red hue. It seems we never have enough of this dressing in my house.

1/4 cup safflower or corn oil

2 1/2 tablespoons toasted sesame oil

1 teaspoon crushed red pepper or 4 to 6 small dried hot chile peppers, cut into 1/4-inch rings and seeded

1 1/2 tablespoons minced garlic

1 tablespoon minced fresh ginger

7 tablespoons soy sauce

3 tablespoons Chinese black vinegar or Worcestershire sauce

2 tablespoons Chinese rice wine or sake

1 1/2 tablespoons sugar

Combine both the oils in a heavy saucepan and heat over high heat until almost smoking hot. Add the red pepper, cover, and remove from the heat. Let sit until cool, about 10 minutes. Add the remaining ingredients and stir to dissolve the sugar. Refrigerated, in a covered container, the dressing will keep for a week.

MAKES ABOUT 1 1/2 CUPS

Chinese Garlic Dressing

THIS ALL-PURPOSE DRESSING CHOCK-FULL OF GARLIC and fresh ginger is wonderful on layered grilled meat and seafood salads or noodle dishes. For a variation, substitute black vinegar or Worcestershire sauce for the clear rice vinegar.

1/4 cup soy sauce

2 tablespoons Japanese rice vinegar

2 tablespoons Chinese rice wine or sake

1 1/2 tablespoons toasted sesame oil

2 tablespoons minced garlic

1 1/2 tablespoons minced fresh ginger

1 tablespoon sugar

1/2 teaspoon crushed red pepper

Combine all the ingredients in a bowl and stir to dissolve the sugar. Refrigerated, in a covered container, the dressing will keep up to a week.

MAKES ABOUT 1 CUP

Spicy Korean Dipping Sauce

KOREAN DRESSINGS USUALLY ARE LIGHT AND SPICY and many share the basic ingredients of soy sauce, dried red pepper powder, and crushed, toasted sesame seeds. Serve this pungent dressing with salads, assorted roll-ups, and grilled meat.

1/2 cup soy sauce

3 1/2 tablespoons Japanese rice vinegar

2 tablespoons water

1 1/2 tablespoons minced fresh ginger

2 teaspoons sugar

2 teaspoons toasted sesame seeds

1 teaspoon crushed red pepper or 1 1/2 teaspoons red pepper powder (available at Asian markets)

In a medium bowl, combine all of the ingredients and mix well. Refrigerated, in a covered container, the sauce will keep for up to a week.

MAKES ABOUT 1 CUP

Spicy Sesame Dressing

DON'T CONFUSE DARK, RICH CHINESE SESAME PASTE with the blander untoasted Middle Eastern tahini paste; the two are not interchangeable. Peanut butter, though, is an acceptable alternative here.

8 cloves garlic, peeled and sliced in half

One 1/2-inch-thick slice fresh ginger, peeled

7 tablespoons Chinese sesame paste, stirred well to blend, or more if necessary

5 tablespoons toasted sesame oil

5 tablespoons soy sauce

1/4 cup Chinese rice wine or sake

1 1/2 tablespoons Chinese black vinegar or Worcestershire sauce

1 1/2 tablespoons sugar

6 tablespoons Chinese Chicken Broth (page 53) or water

In a food processor fitted with the metal blade or in a blender, finely chop the garlic and ginger. Add the remaining ingredients in the order listed and process to blend. The dressing should be the consistency of heavy cream. If it is too thin, add up to 2 tablespoons additional sesame paste. Refrigerated, in a covered container, the dressing will keep for up to a week.

MAKES ABOUT 2 CUPS

Mongolian Sauce

THIS FLAVORFUL HOT-AND-SOUR SAUCE IS ONE of my all-time favorites. Traditionally it is served with Mongolian Firepot, a fondue-style meat or soup (see Seafood Hot Pot, page 62). I, however, use it in any type of seafood casserole. It also accentuates the fresh, sweet flavor of the seafood.

3/4 cup soy sauce

3 1/2 tablespoons Chinese rice wine or sake

3 1/2 tablespoons Chinese black vinegar or Worcestershire sauce

3 tablespoons minced scallions

2 tablespoons minced fresh ginger

2 tablespoons minced garlic

2 tablespoons sugar

1 teaspoon hot chile paste (optional)

Combine all the ingredients in a bowl and stir to dissolve the sugar. Refrigerated, in a covered container, the dressing will keep for a week.

MAKES ABOUT 13/4 CUPS

Cilantro Vinaigrette

CILANTRO IS A HEADY HERB THAT COMPLEMENTS the flavors of fresh vegetables, seafood, and chicken. I make batches of this dressing, store it in the refrigerator, and add the fresh cilantro just before serving the dish.

1/3 cup soy sauce

1/4 cup Japanese rice vinegar

3 tablespoons toasted sesame oil

1 1/2 tablespoons Chinese rice wine or sake

1 1/2 tablespoons sugar

1/3 cup chopped fresh cilantro

In a medium bowl, combine all the ingredients except the cilantro and stir to dissolve the sugar. Just before serving, stir in the cilantro. Refrigerated, in a covered container, the vinaigrette will keep up to a week.

MAKES ABOUT 1 CUP

Chinese Peanut Dressing

MY REFRIGERATOR WOULD SEEM EMPTY without a batch of this all-purpose peanut butter–based sauce. I serve it with vegetable and noodle salads, and as a go-with-anything dipping sauce.

One 1/2-inch-thick slice fresh ginger, peeled and sliced in half

8 cloves garlic, peeled

1 teaspoon hot chile paste, or more to taste

1/2 cup smooth peanut butter, or more if necessary

1/4 cup soy sauce

3 1/2 tablespoons sugar

3 1/2 tablespoons Chinese black vinegar or Worcestershire sauce

3 tablespoons toasted sesame oil

5 tablespoons Chinese Chicken Broth (page 53) or water, or more if necessary

In a food processor fitted with the metal blade or in a blender, finely chop the ginger and garlic. Add the remaining ingredients in the order listed and process until smooth. The dressing should be the consistency of heavy cream. If it is too thick, add more water or chicken broth; if too thin, add more peanut butter. Refrigerated, in a covered container, the dressing will keep for 2 to 3 weeks.

MAKES ABOUT 13/4 CUPS

Korean Sesame Dressing

MANY AMERICANS ARE UNFAMILIAR WITH the deliciously spicy, sweet, and sour dressings favored by Korean cooks. This one, with the addition of garlic and hot chile paste, is a classic.

6 tablespoons toasted sesame oil

4 1/2 tablespoons Japanese rice vinegar

3 tablespoons mirin (sweetened rice wine)

1/4 cup crushed toasted sesame seeds

2 tablespoons minced garlic

1 tablespoon sugar

2 tablespoons hot chile paste, or to taste

Combine all the ingredients in a bowl and stir to dissolve the sugar. Refrigerated, in a covered container, the dressing will keep up to a week.

MAKES ABOUT 1 CUP

127

129

130

131